Tattoo
COLORING BOOK

This Book Belongs to:

_____
_____

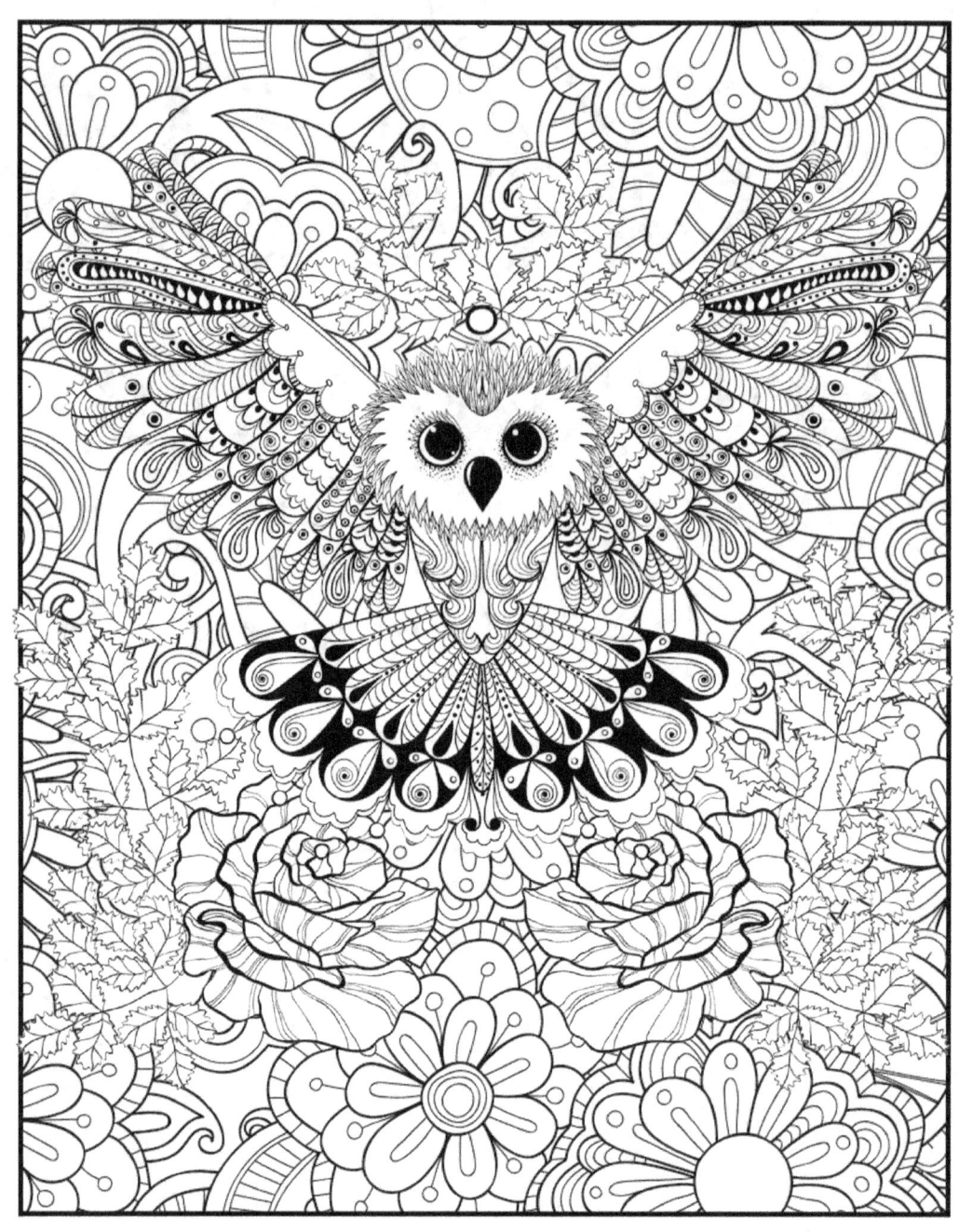

ALL RIGHT RESERVED

No part of this book may be reproduced,stored in a retrieval system,or transmitted in any foram or by any means,electronic,mechanical, photocopying,recording,scanning,or otherwise,without the prior written permission of the publisher

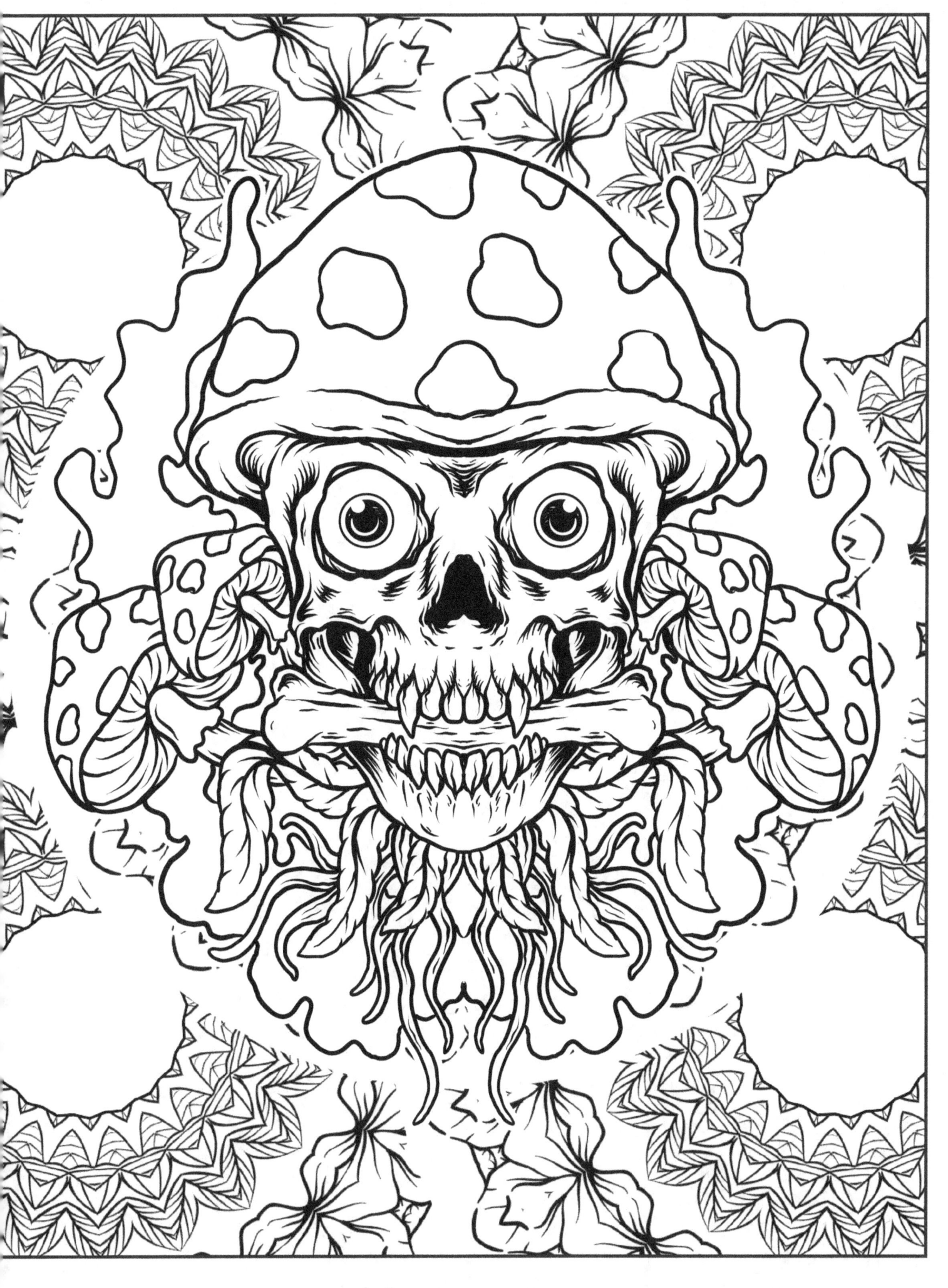

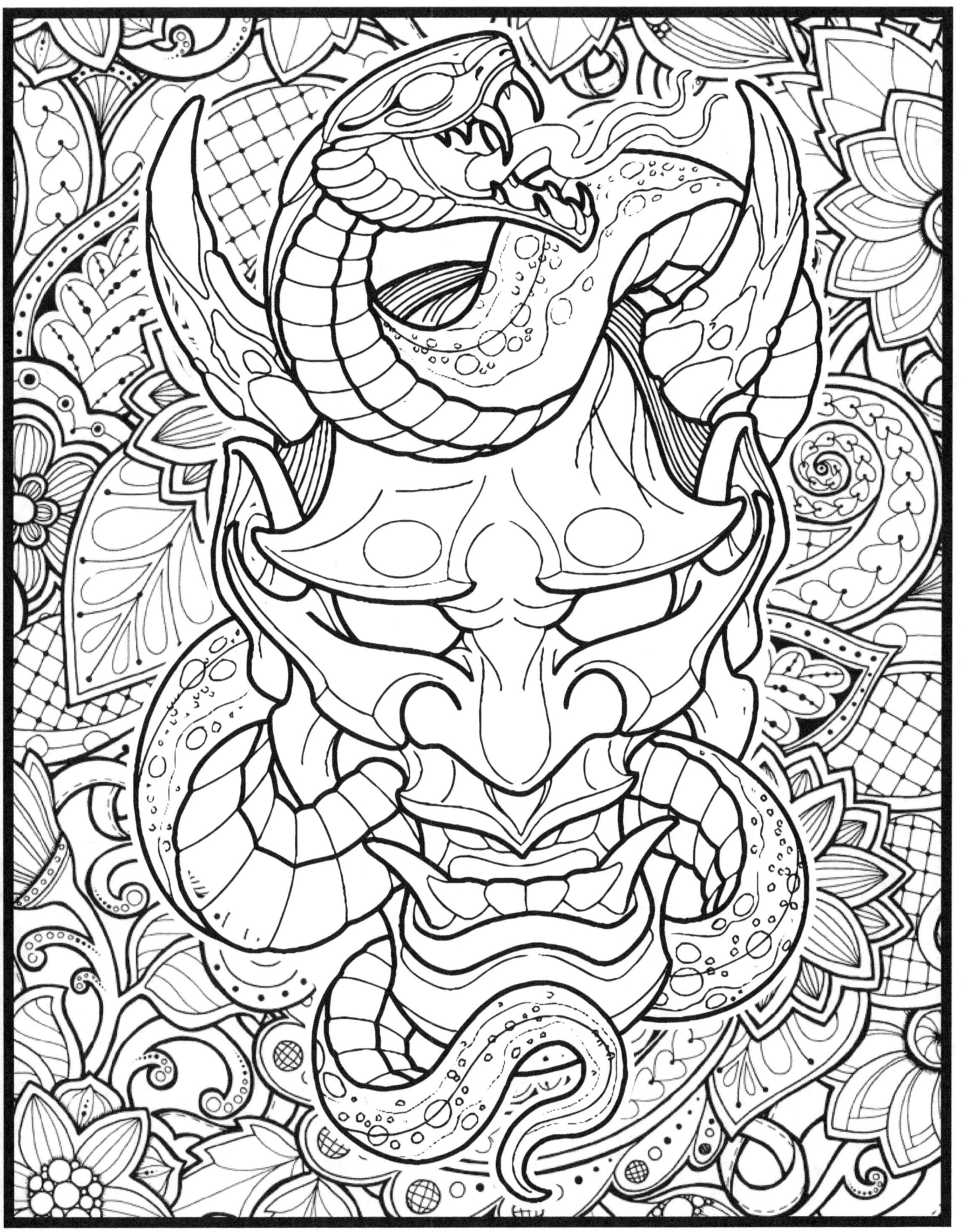

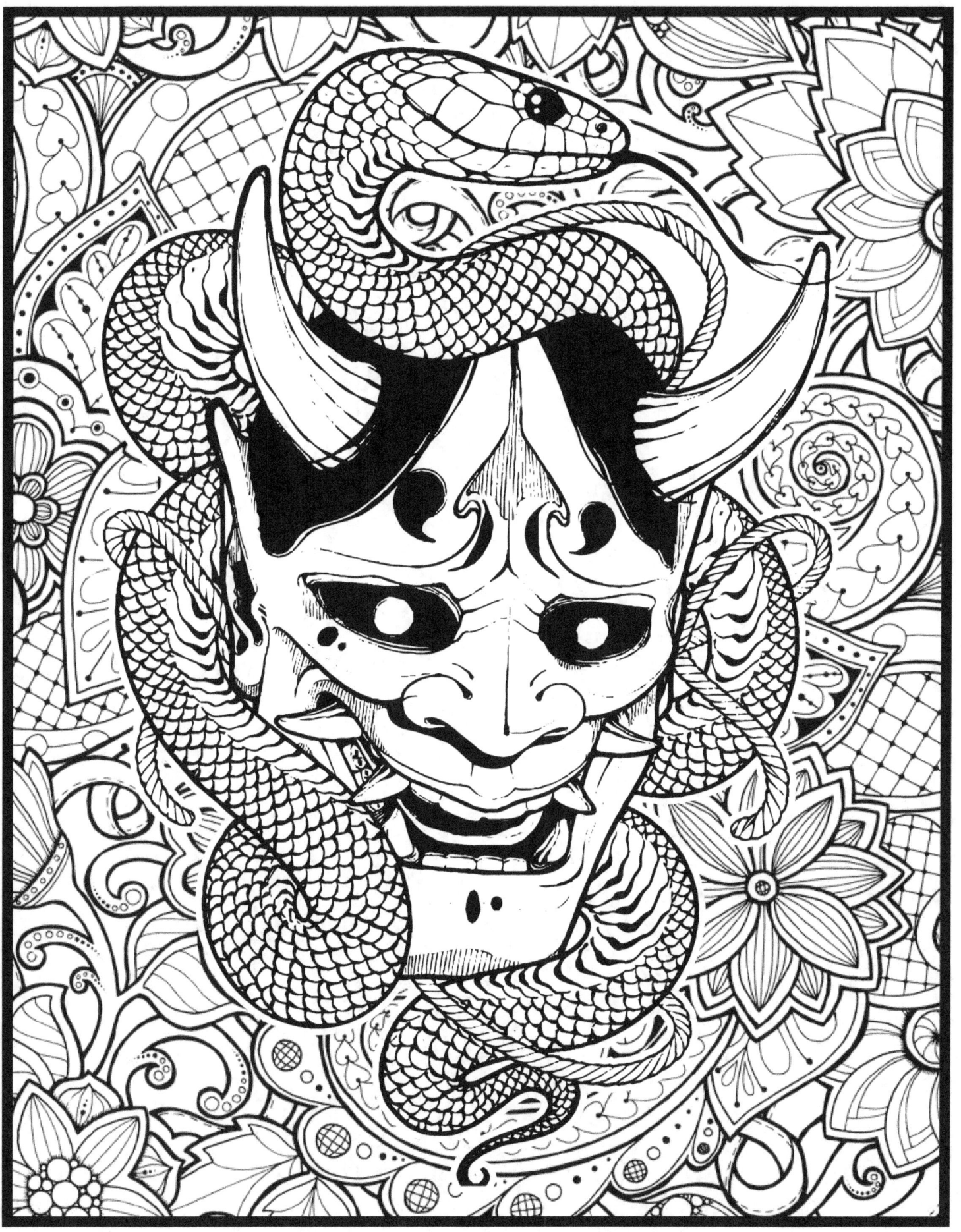

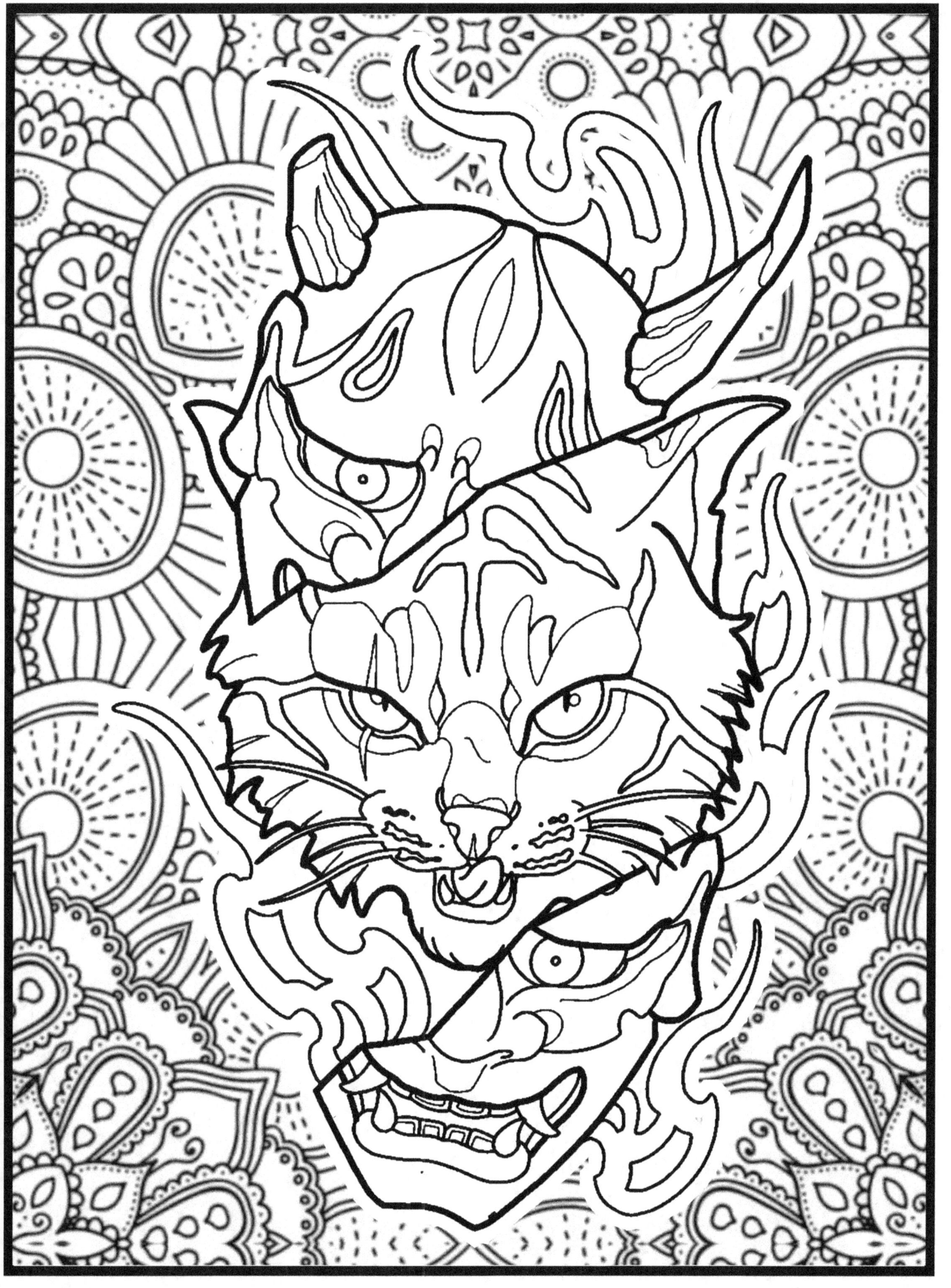

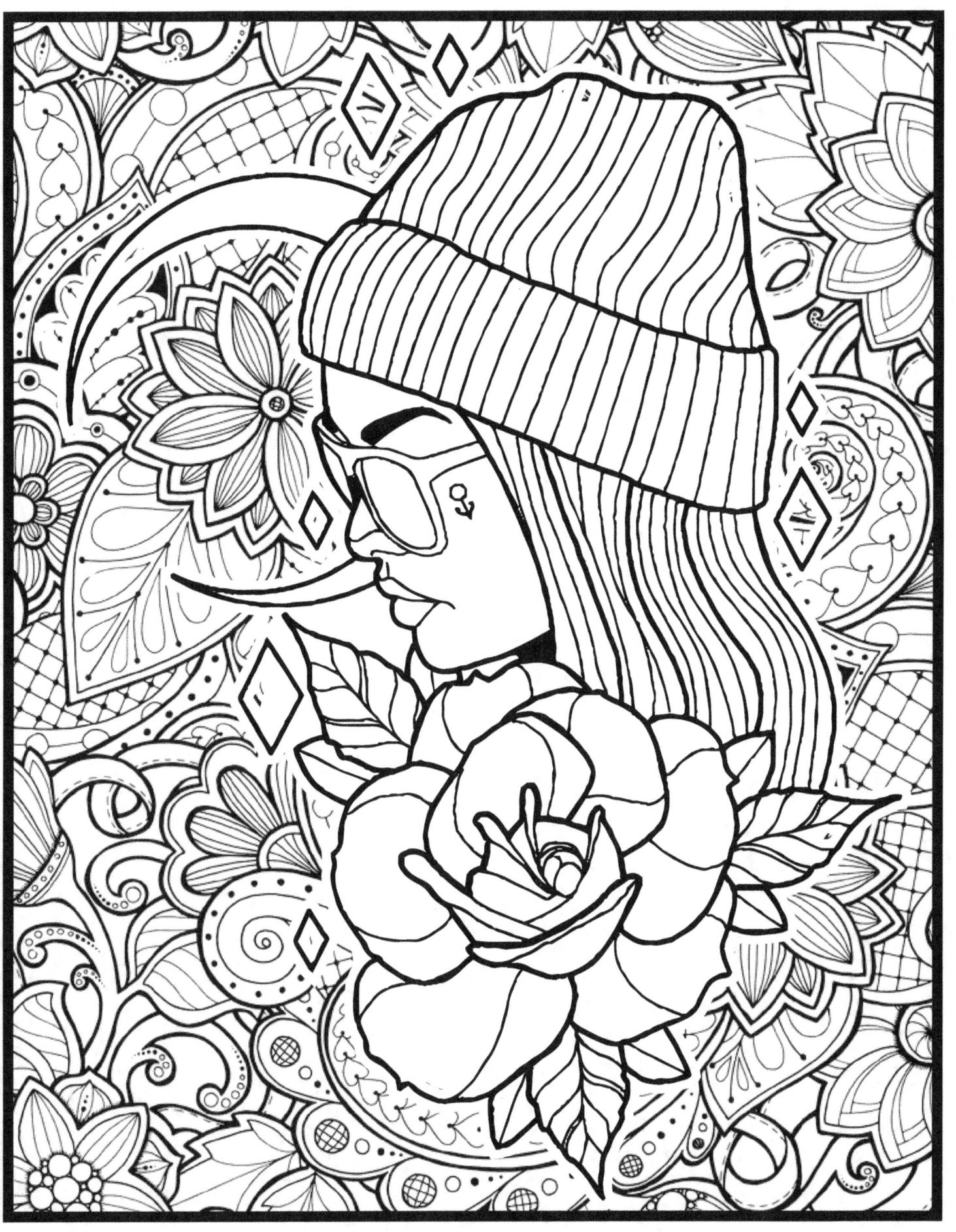

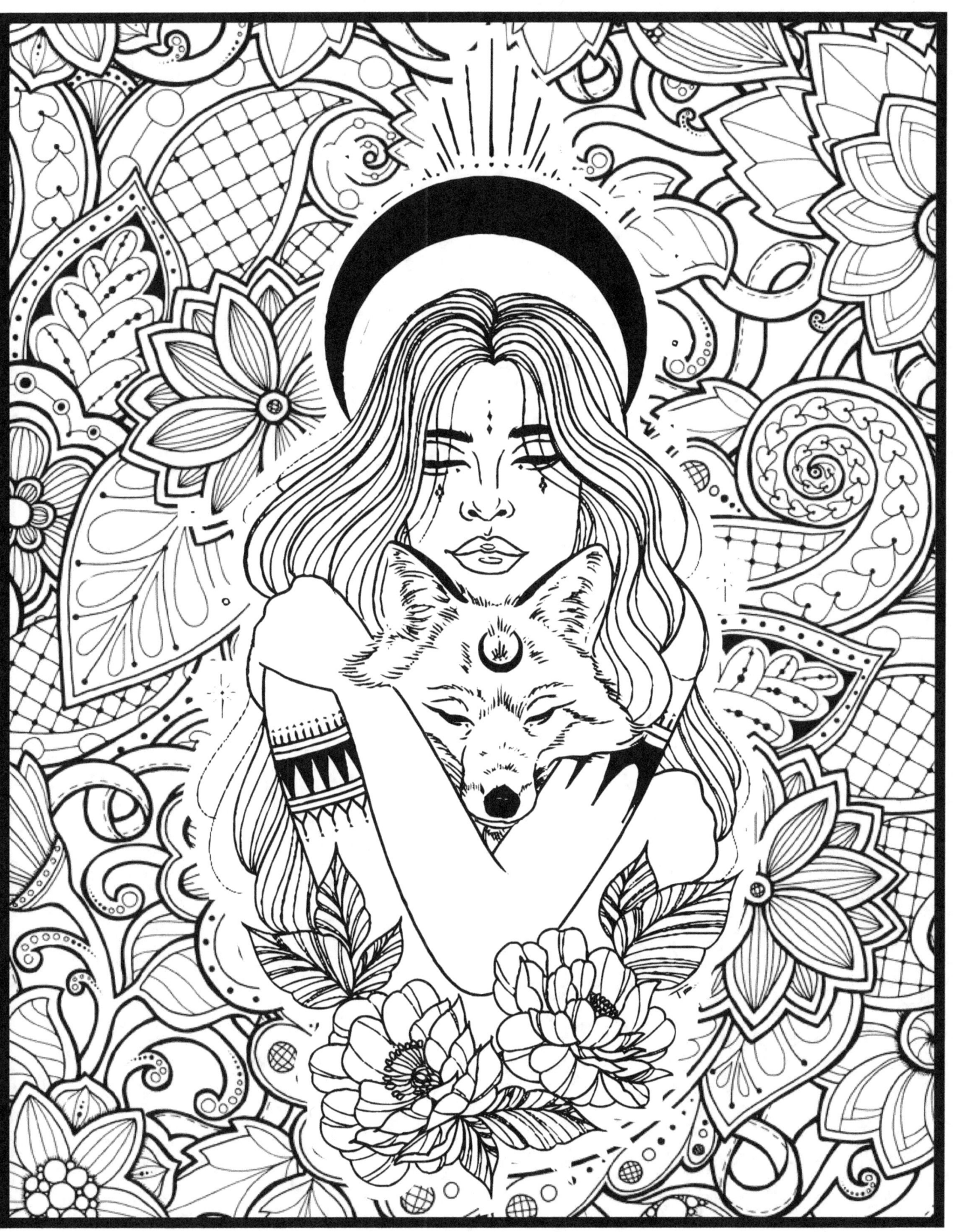

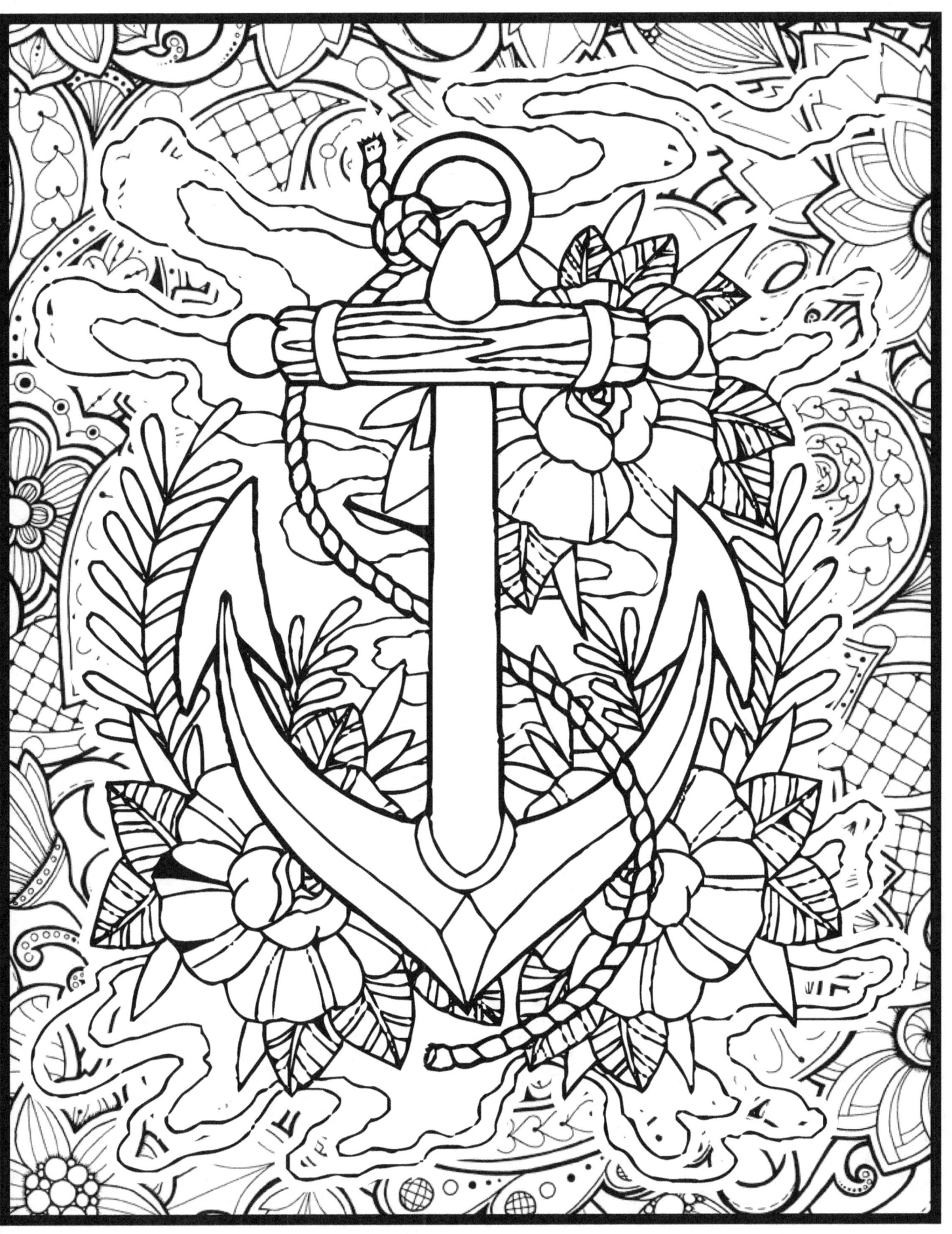

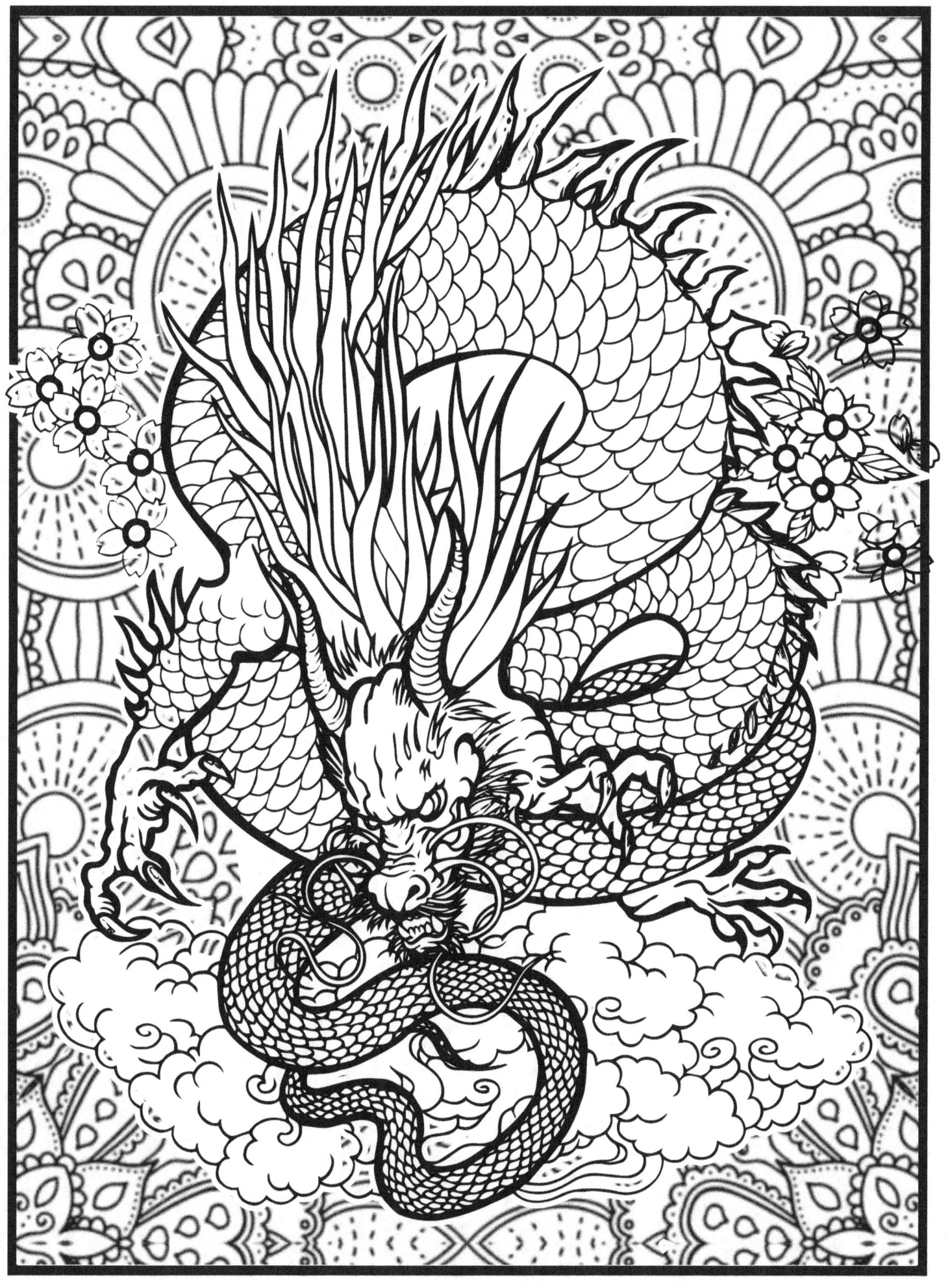

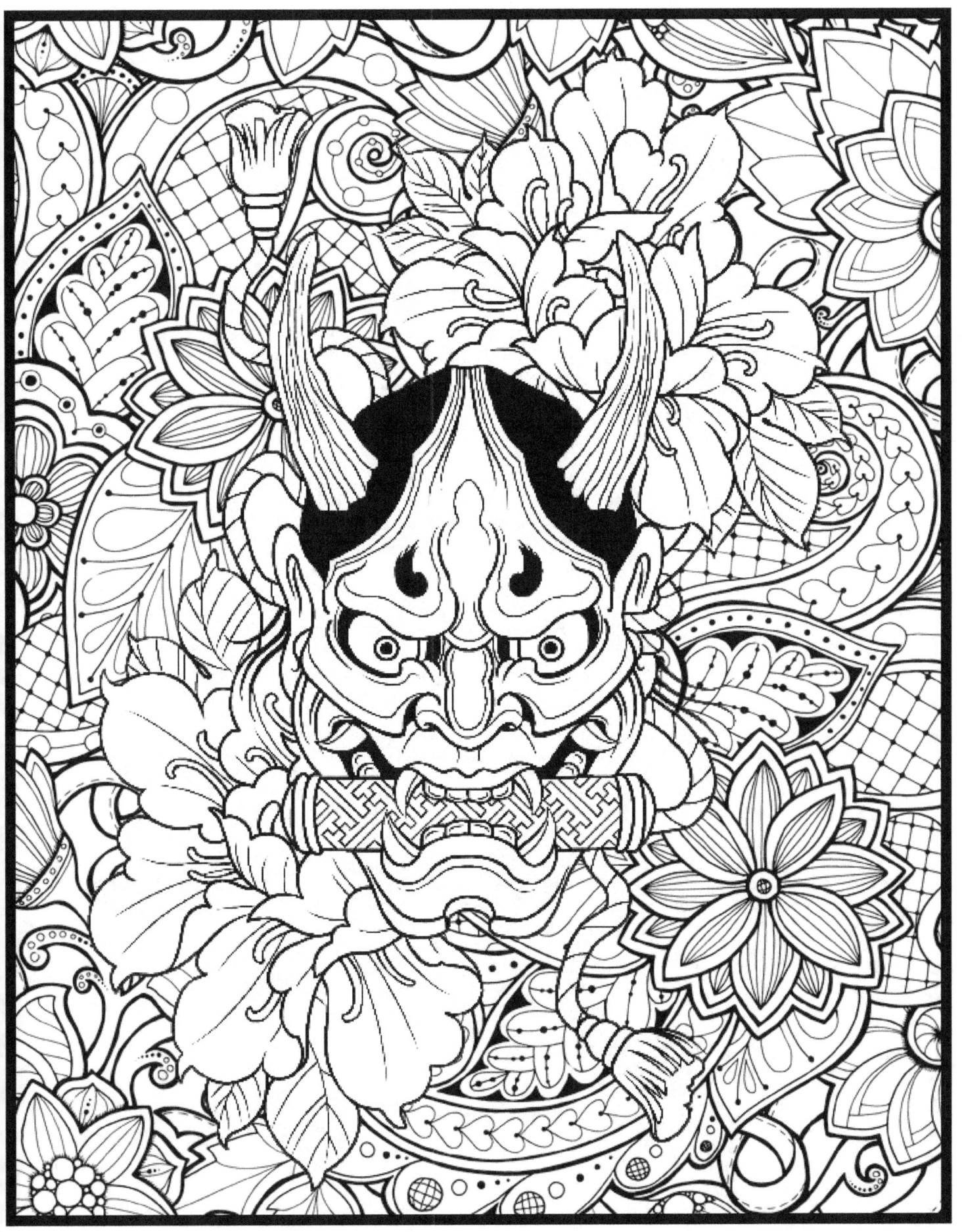

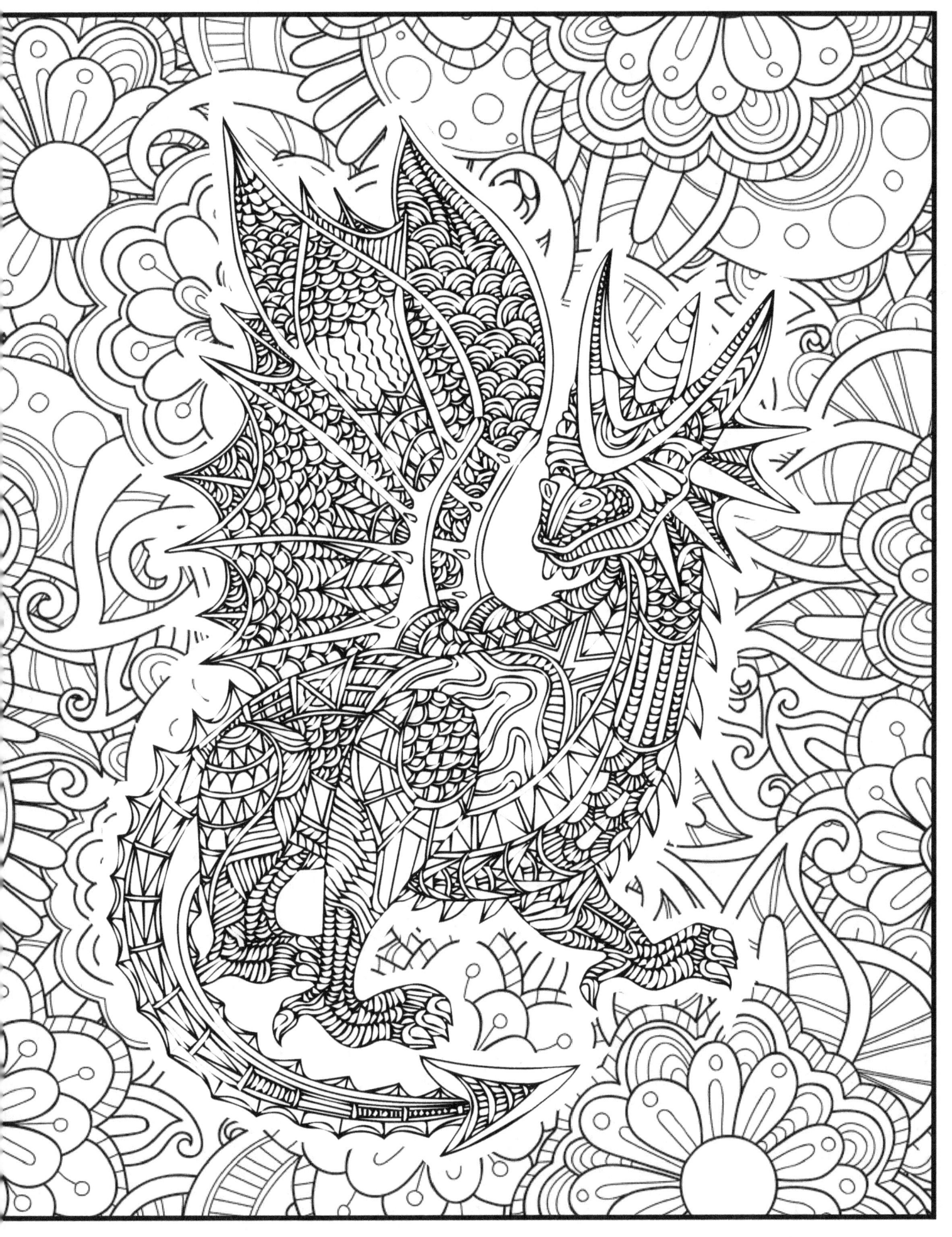

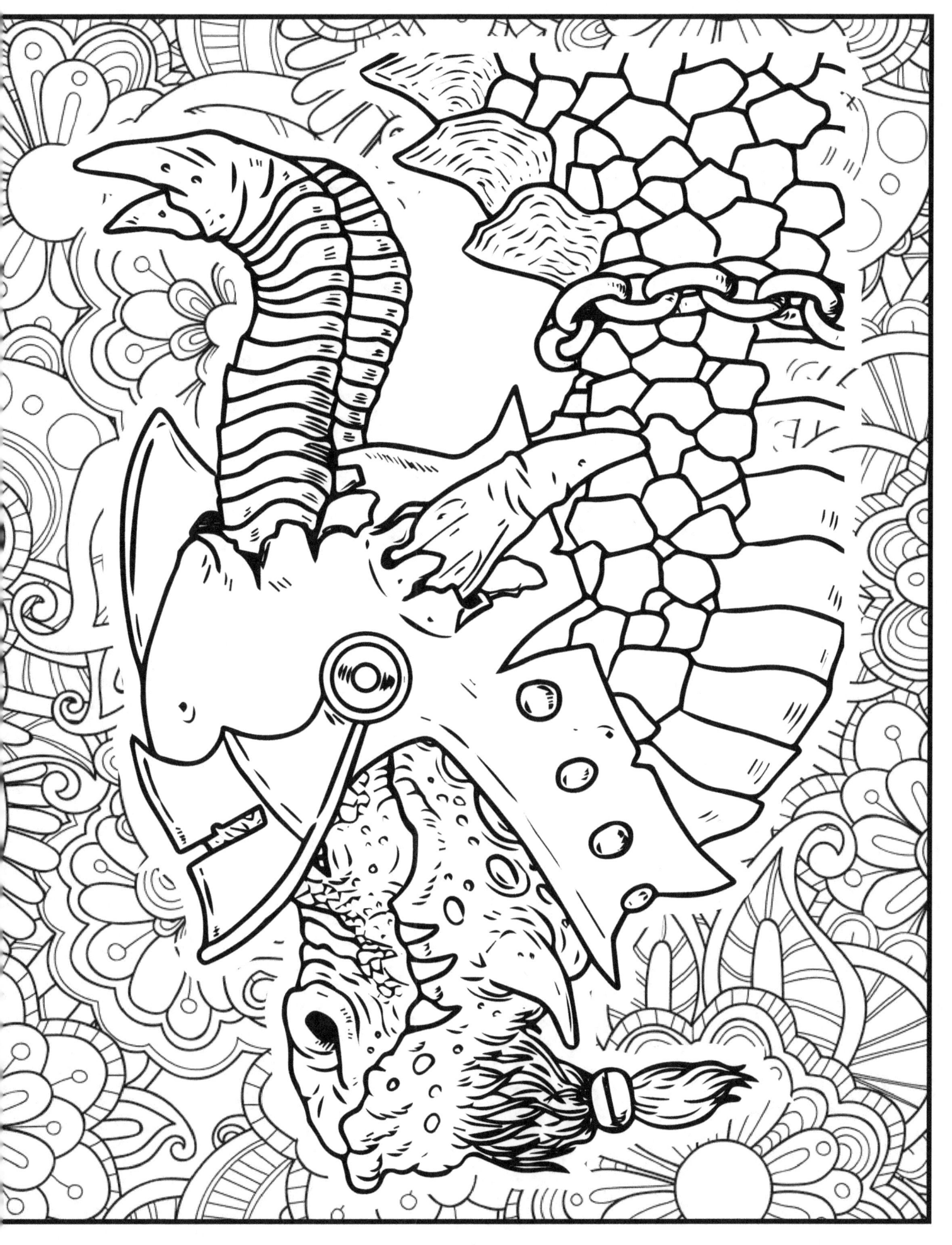

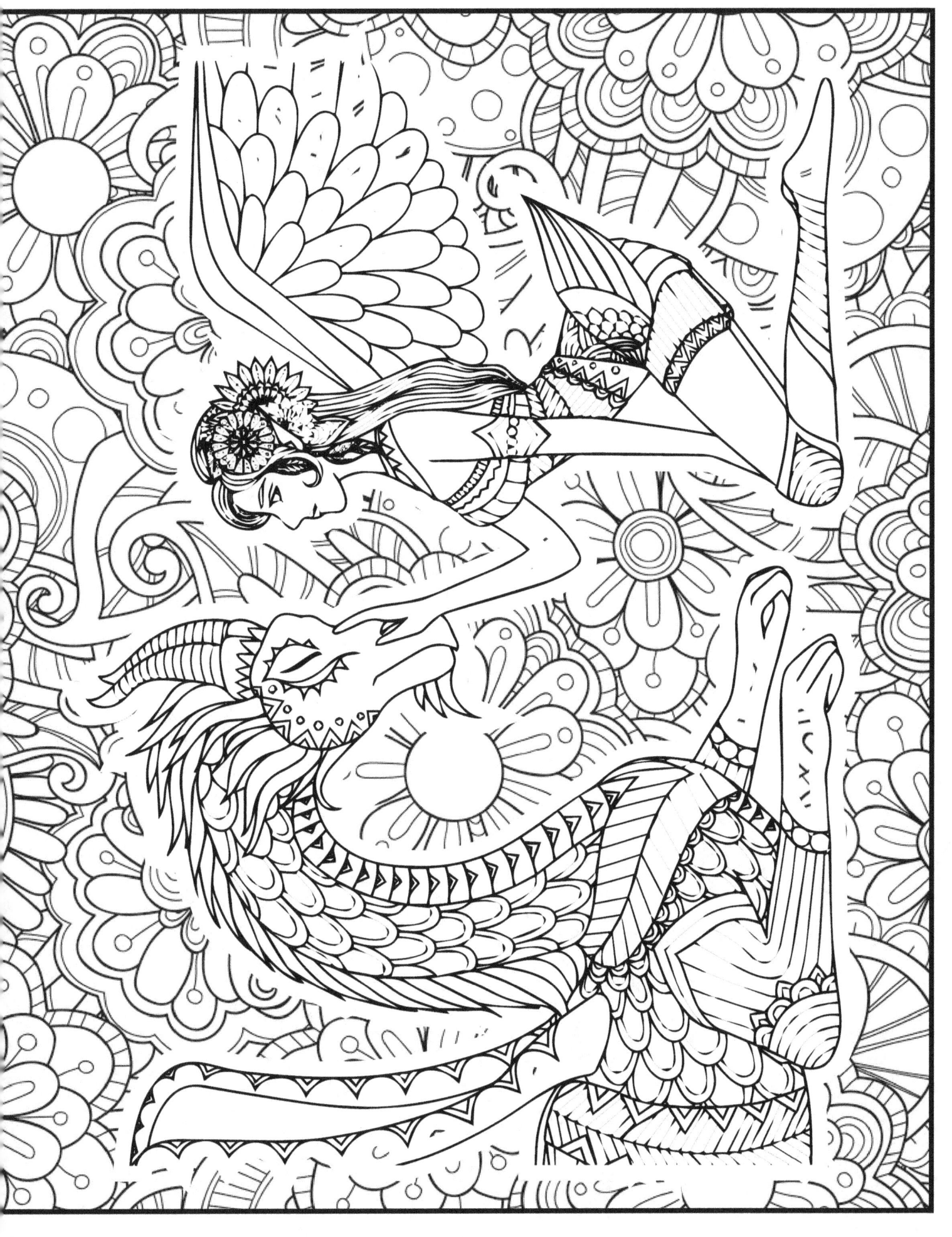

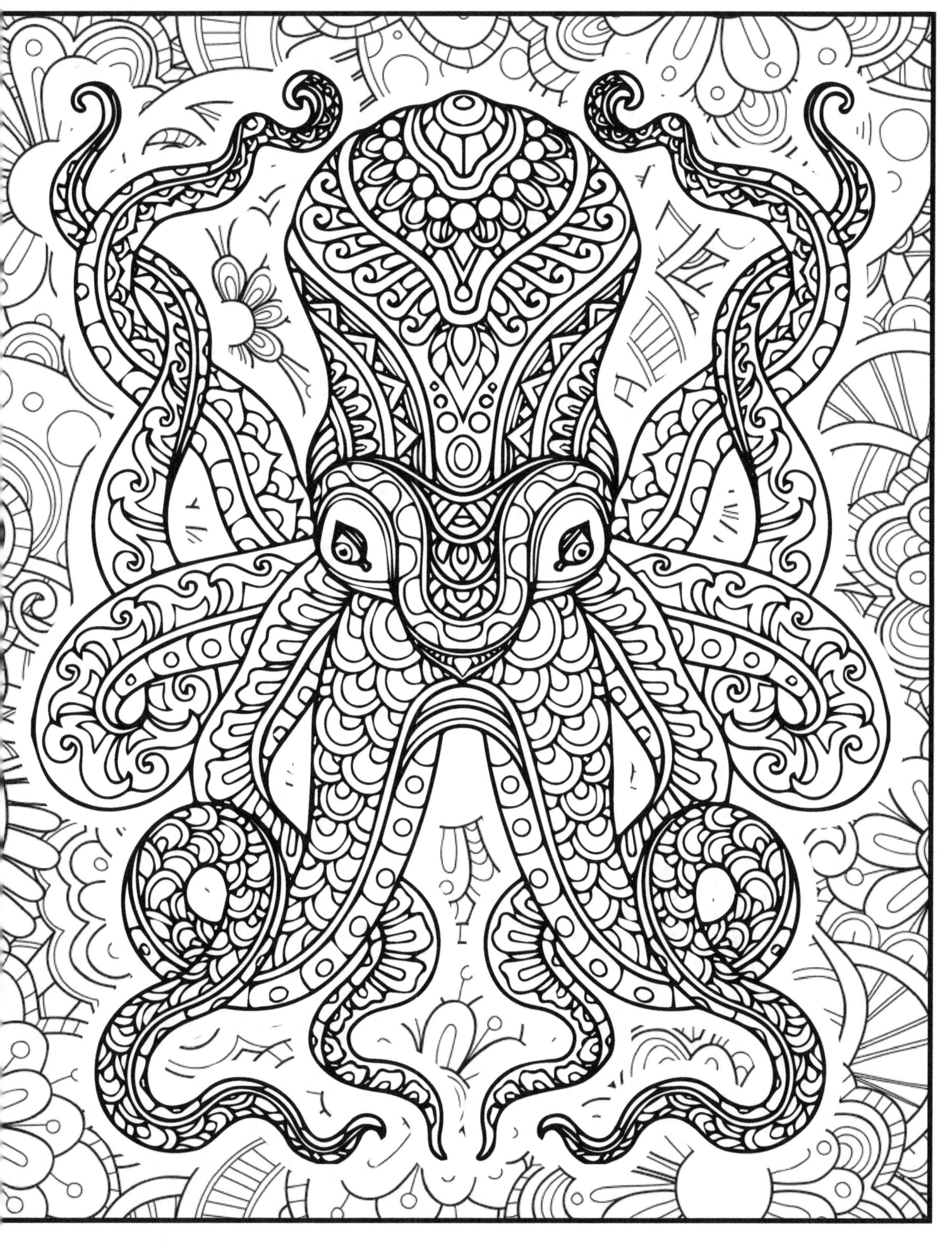

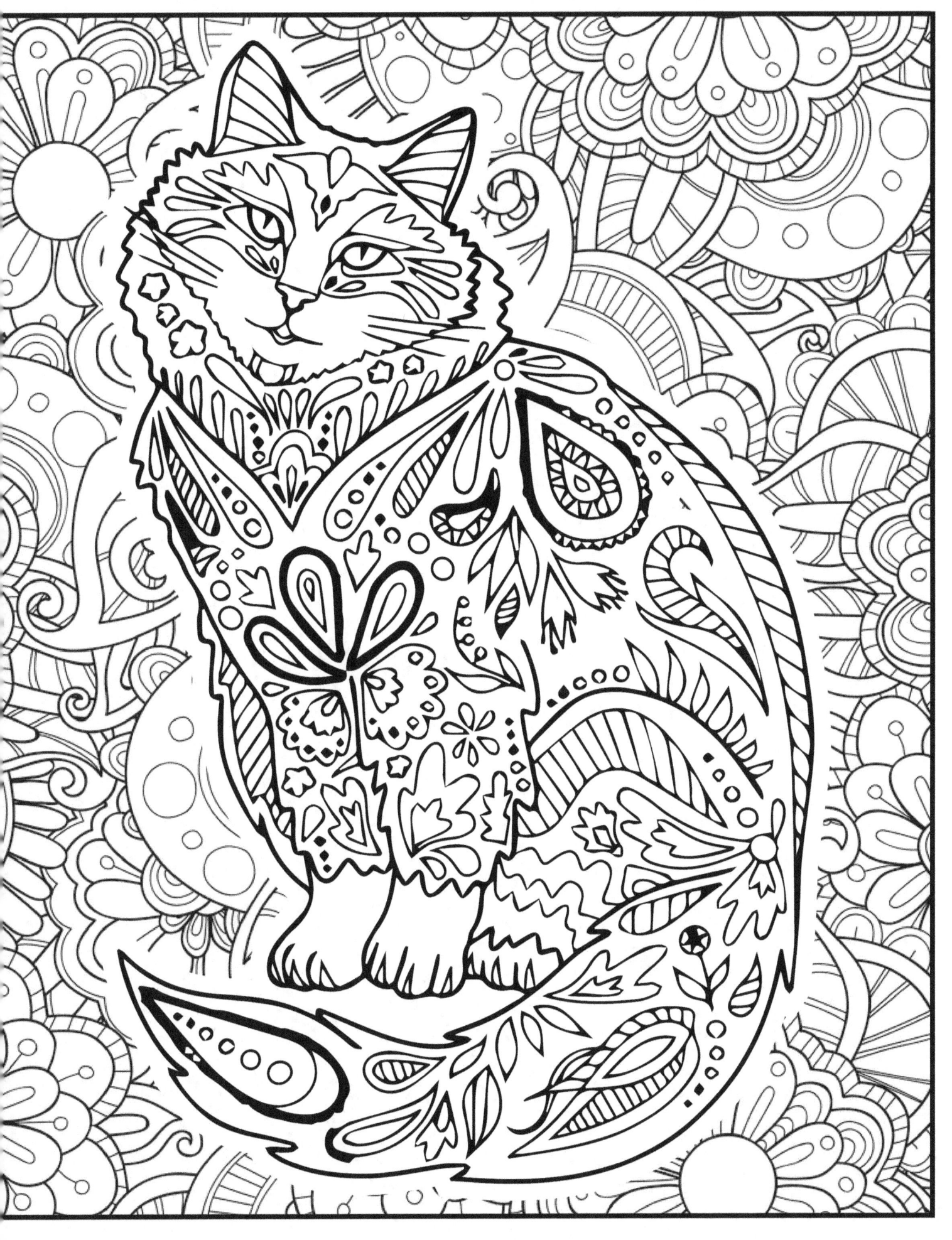

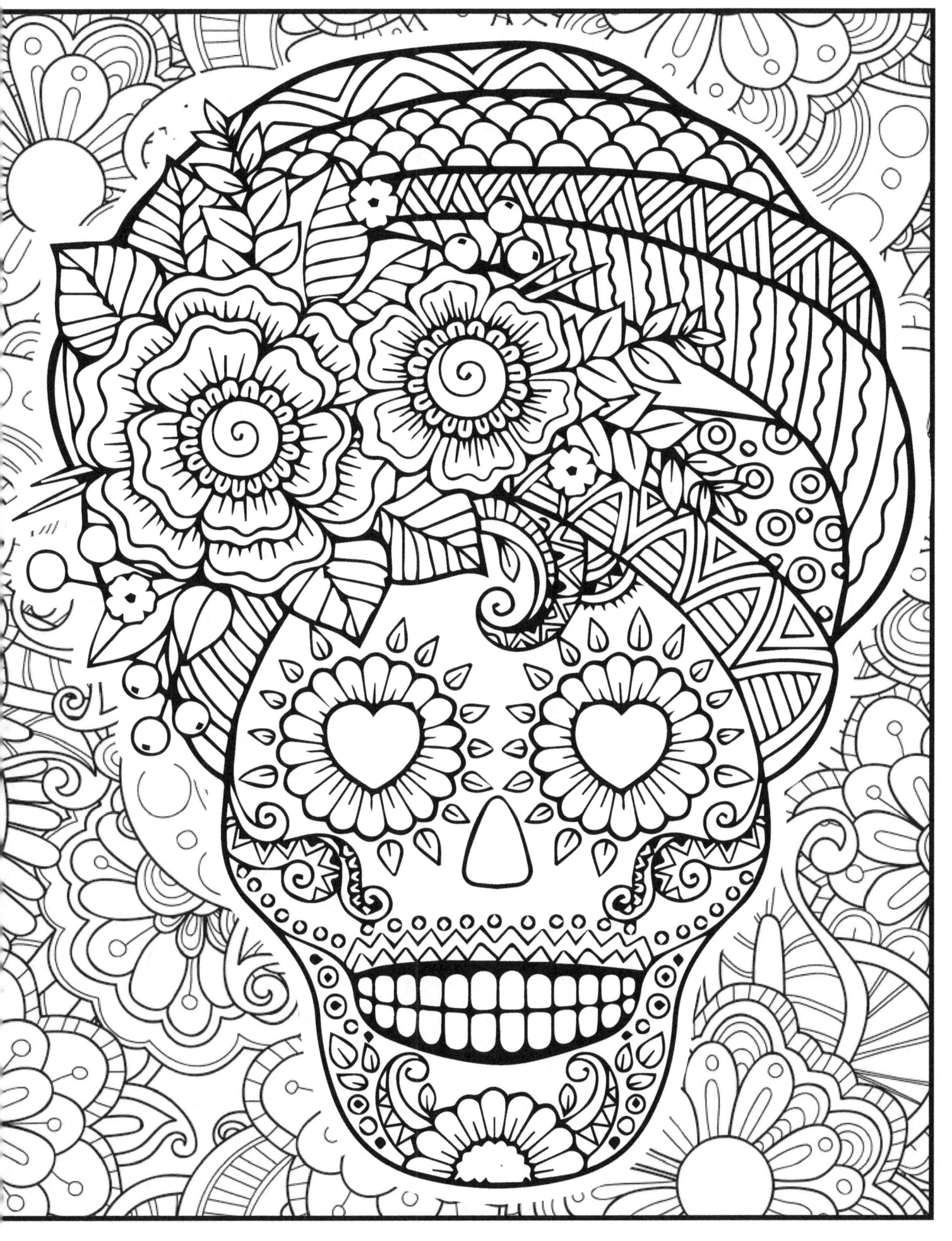

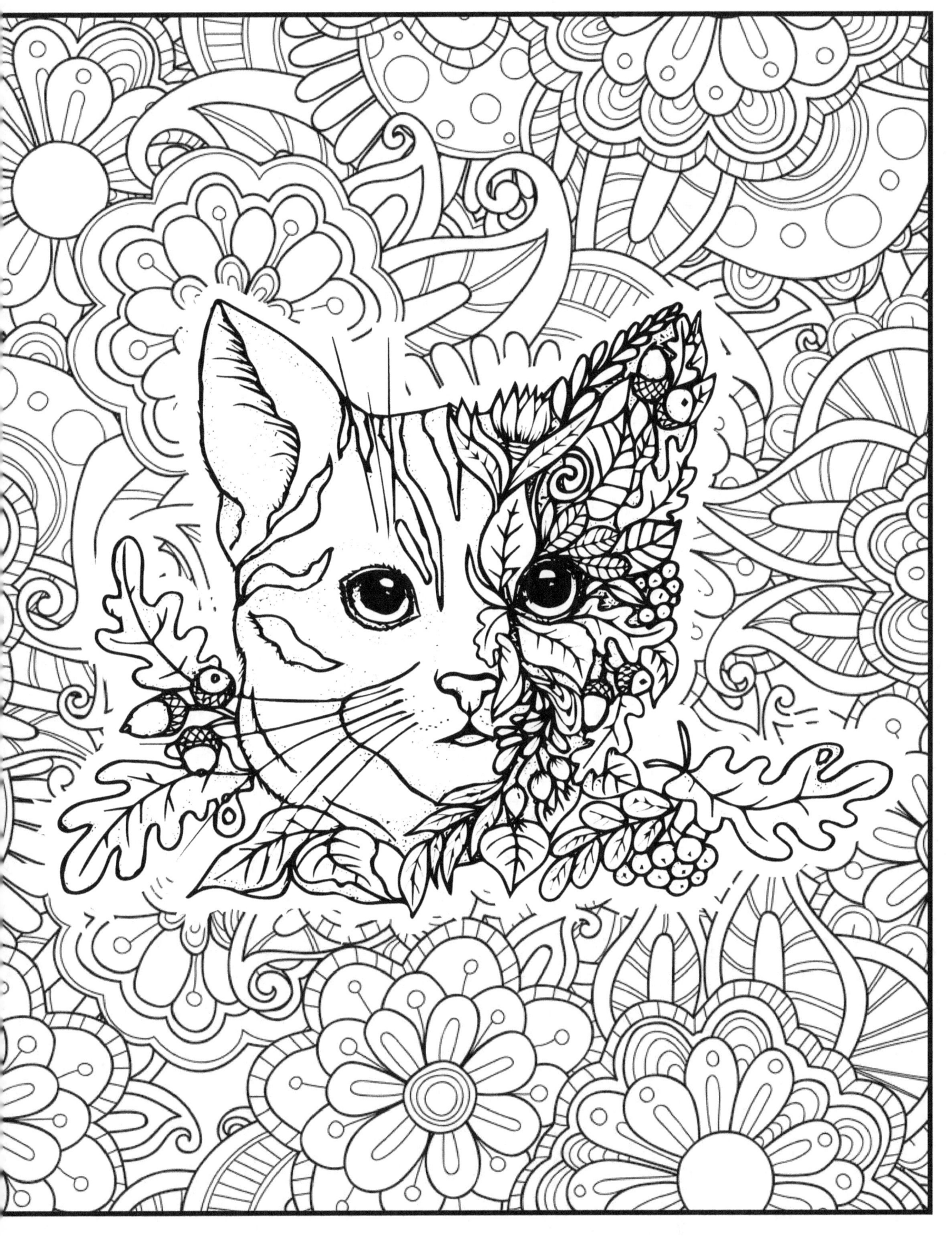

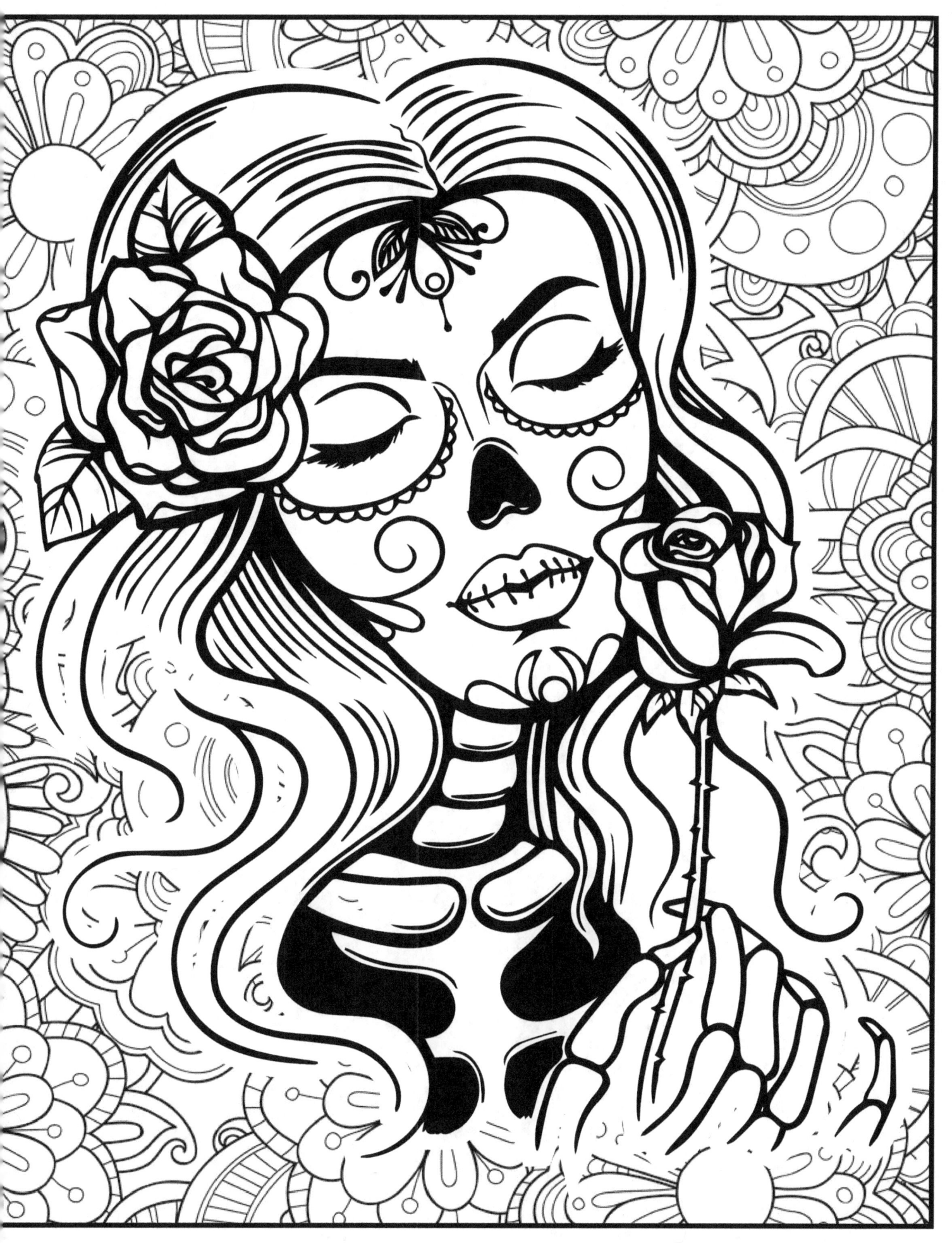

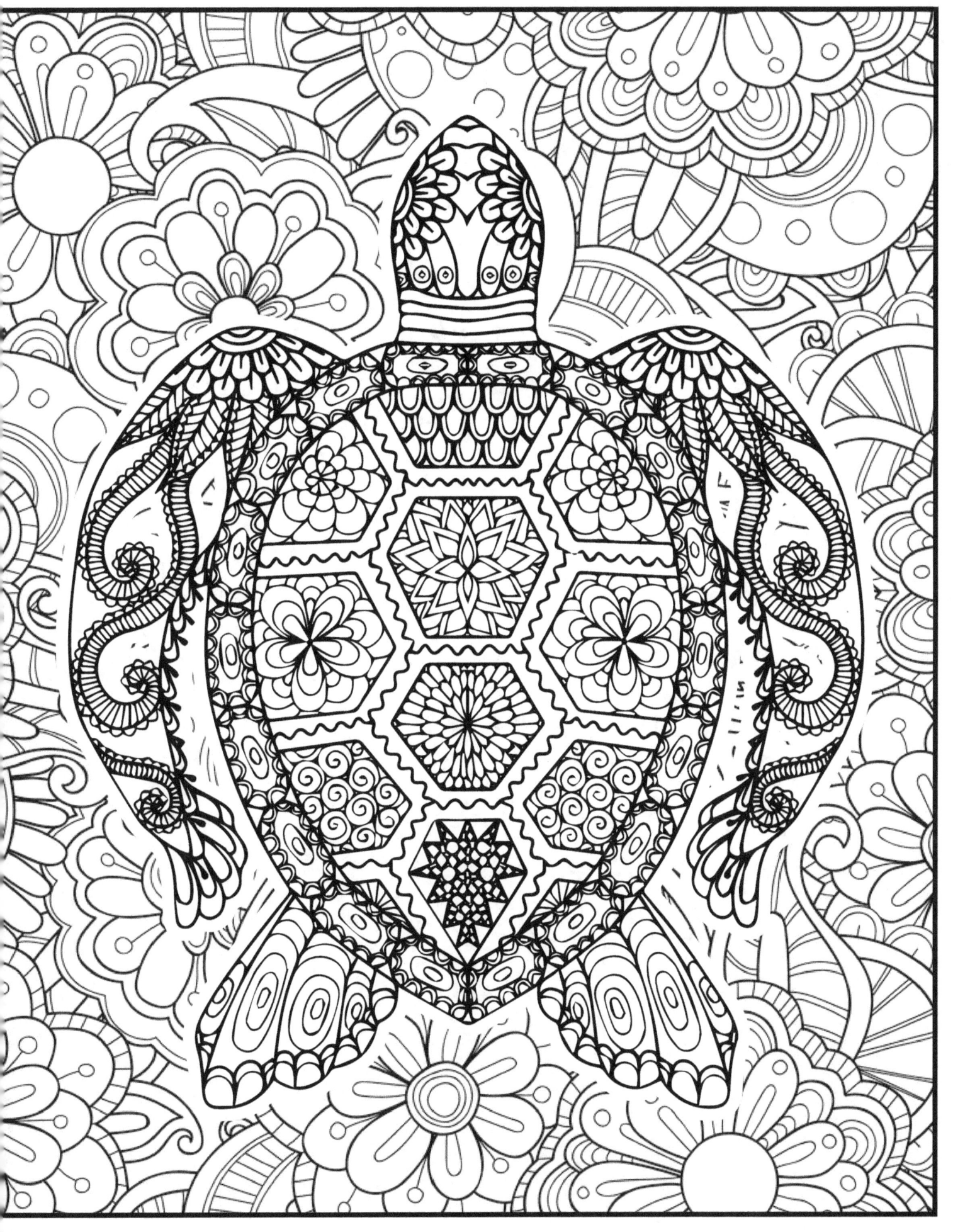

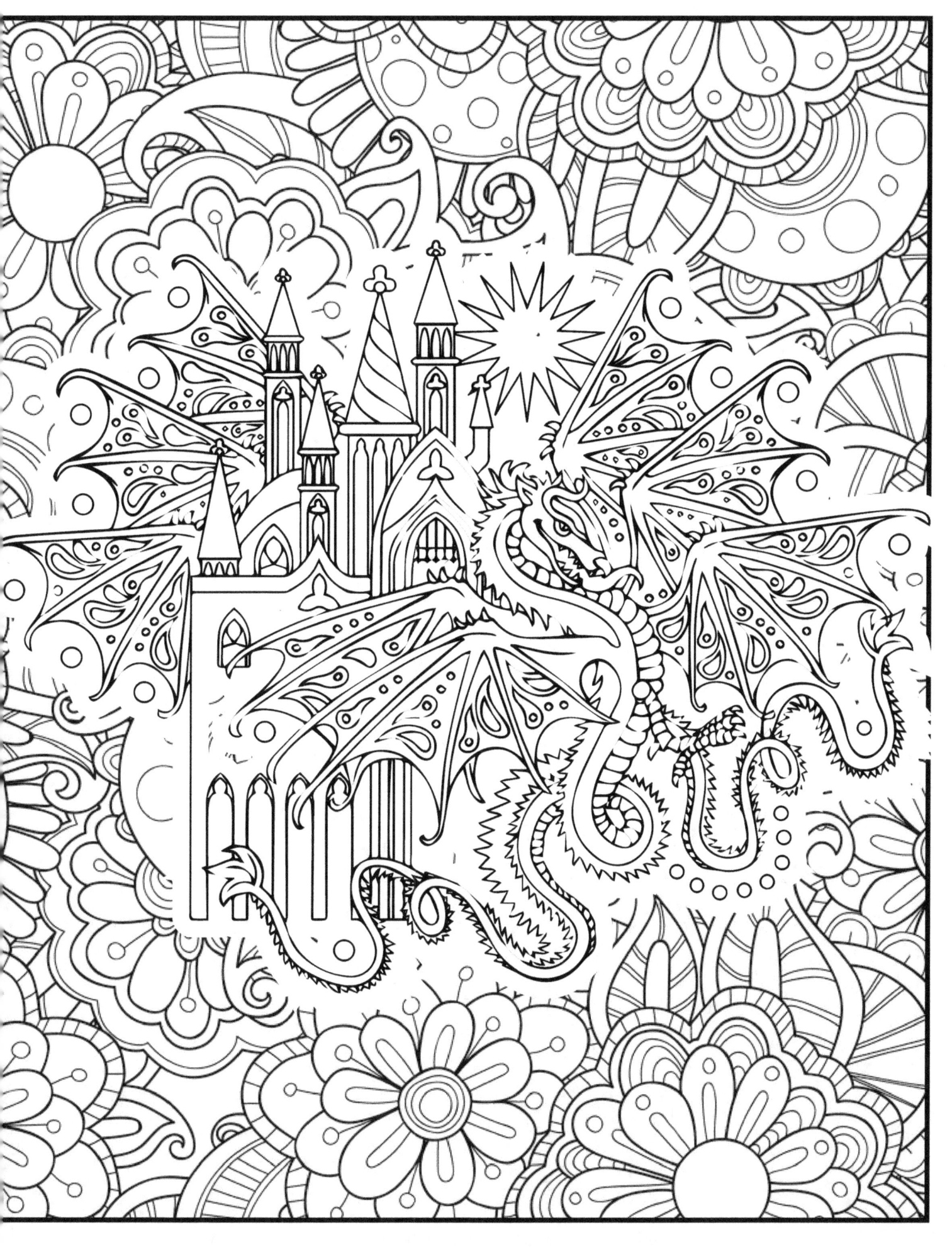

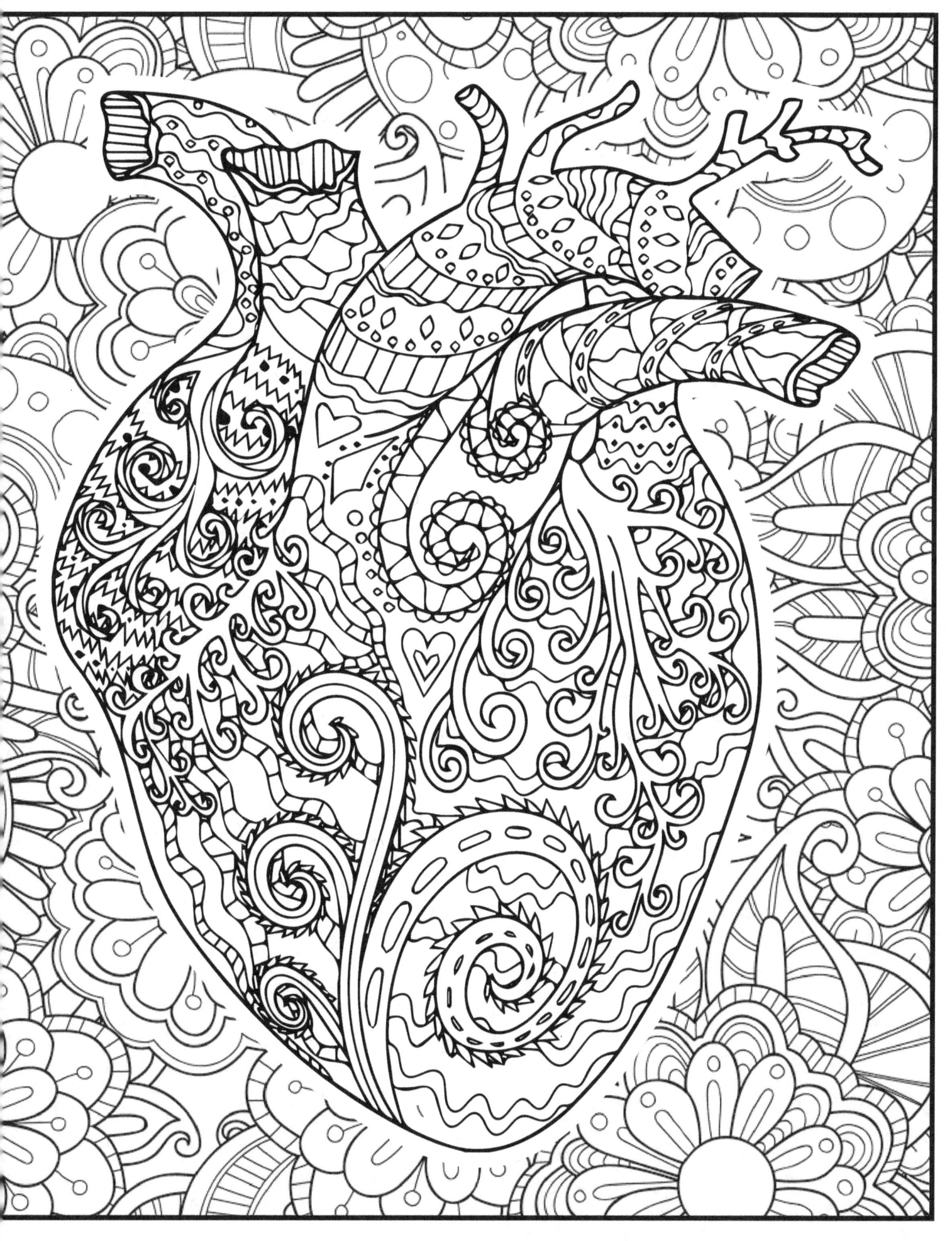

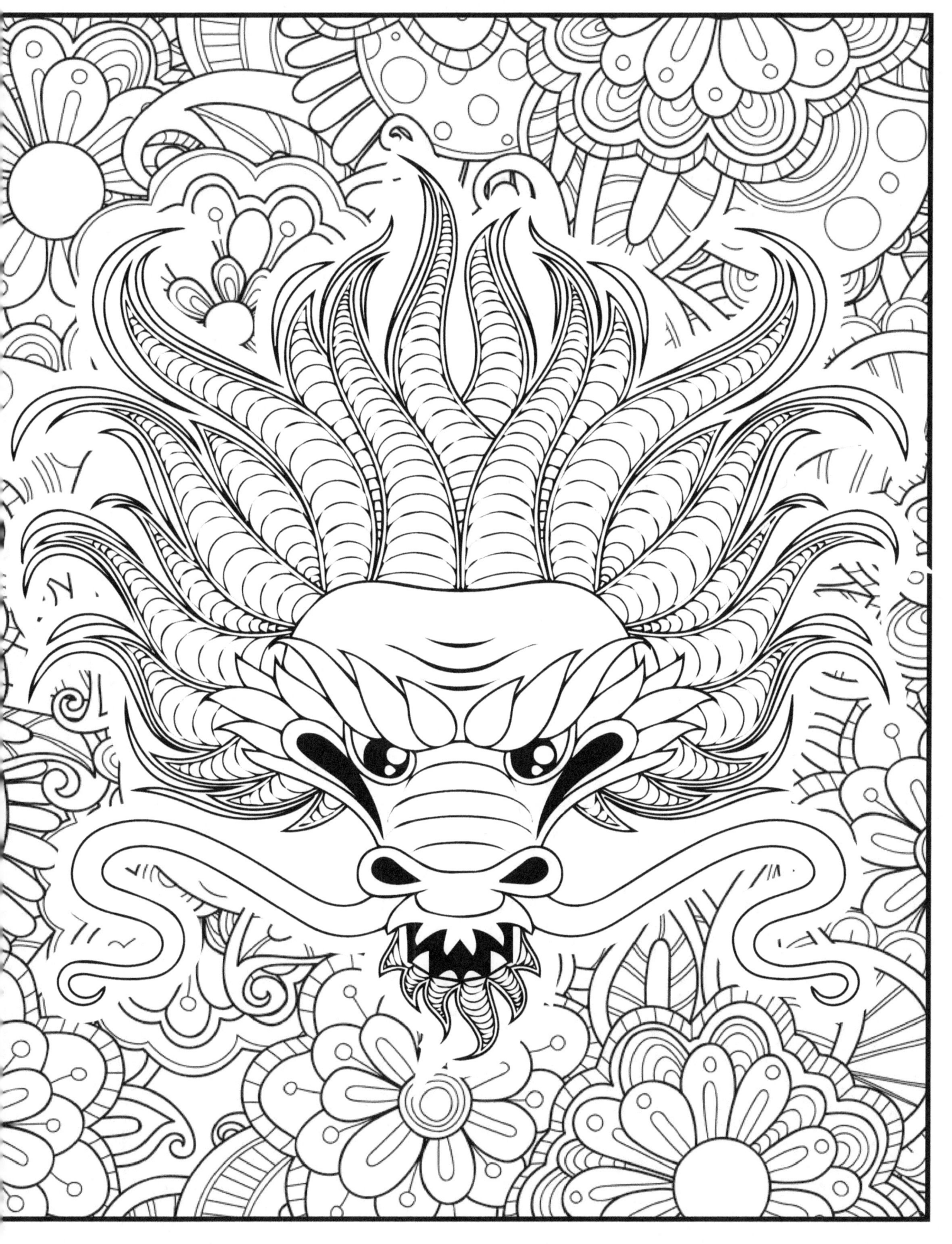

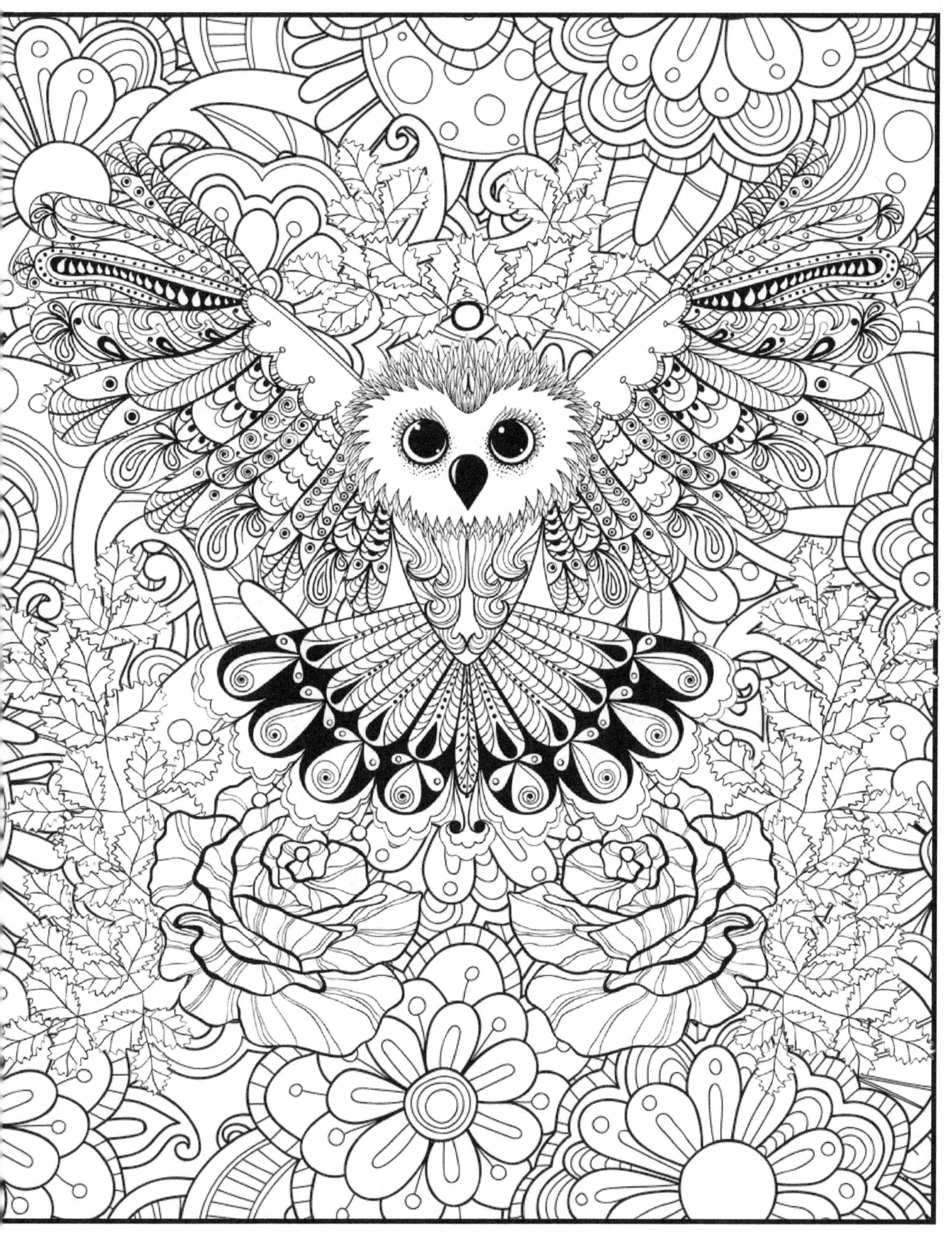

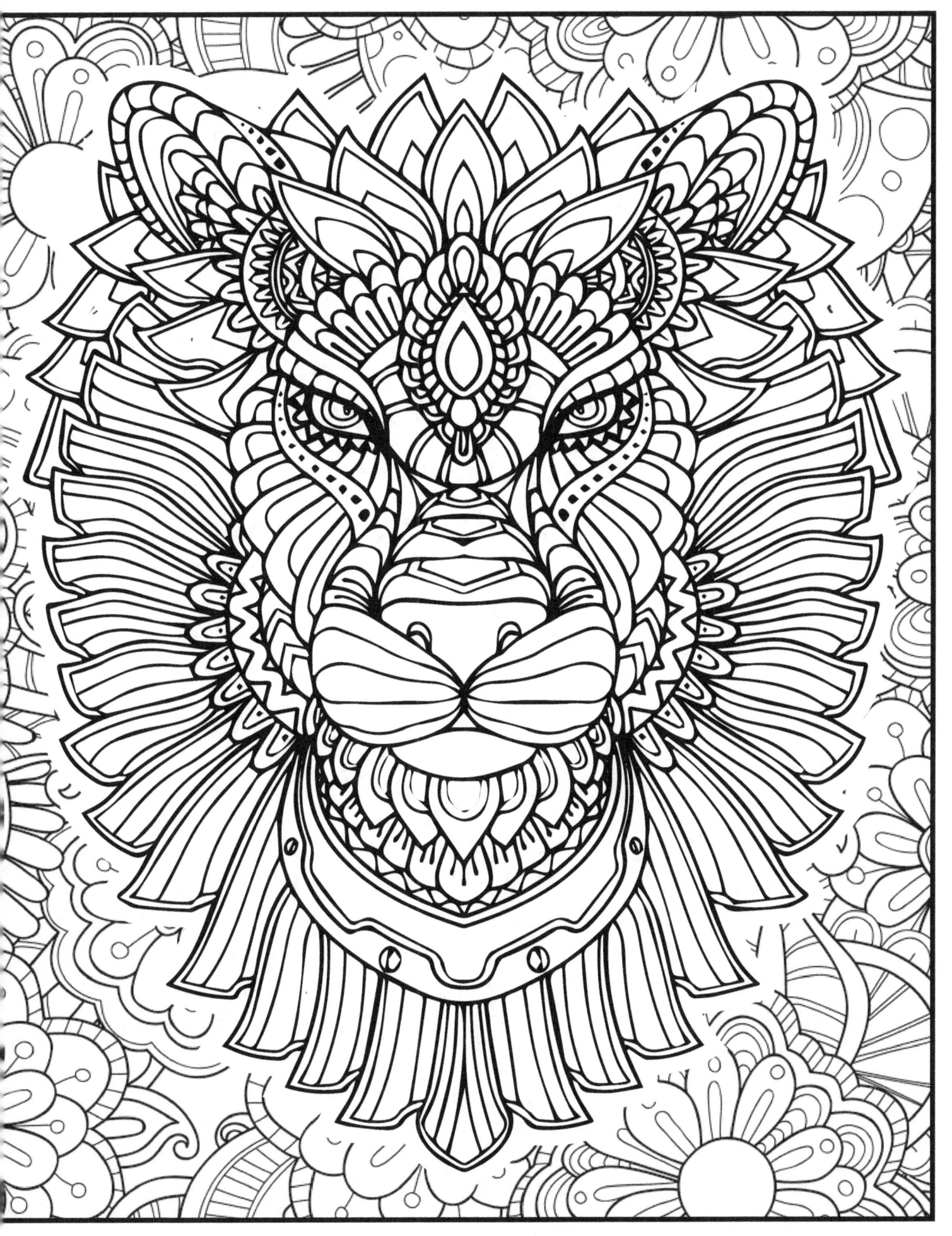

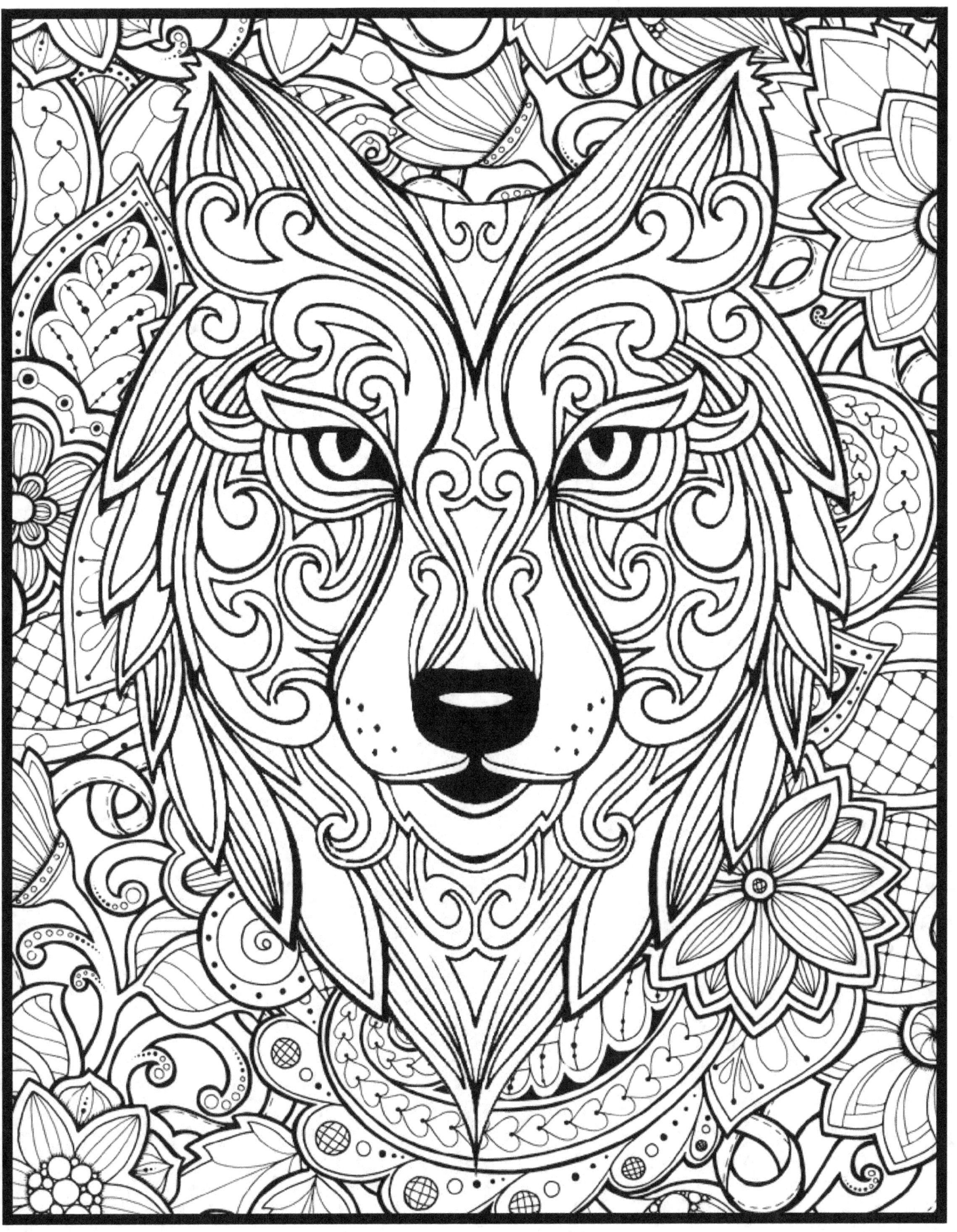

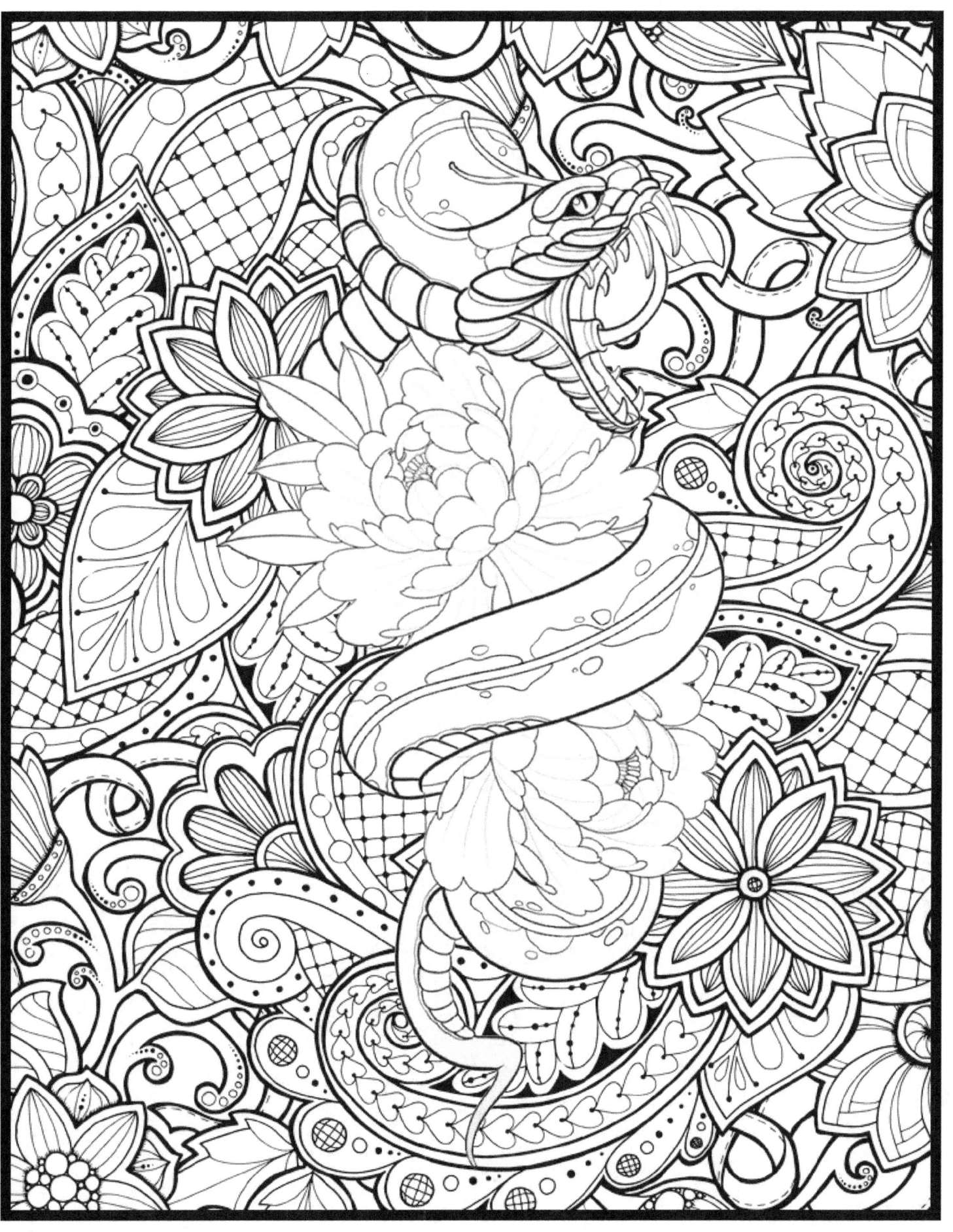

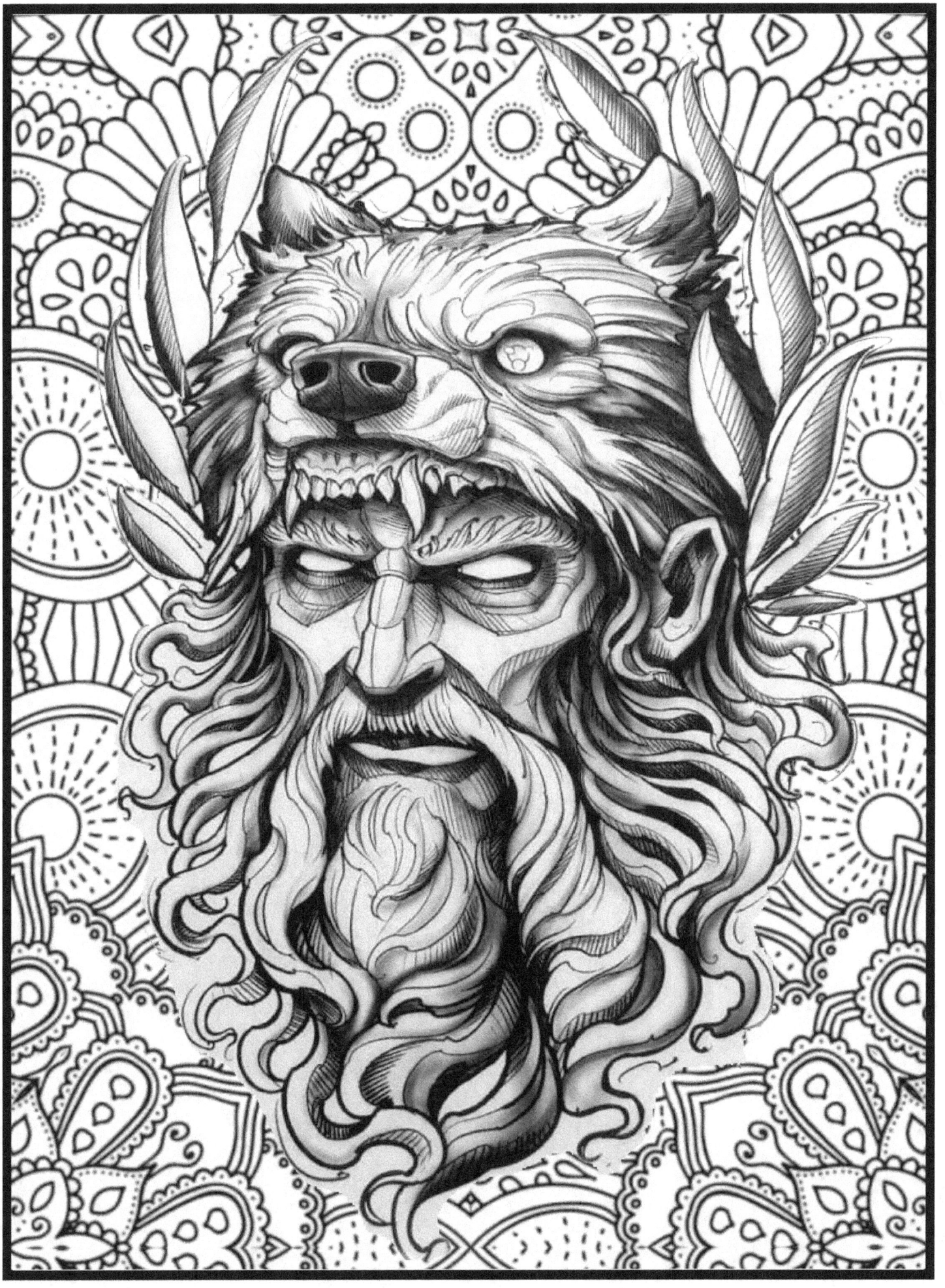

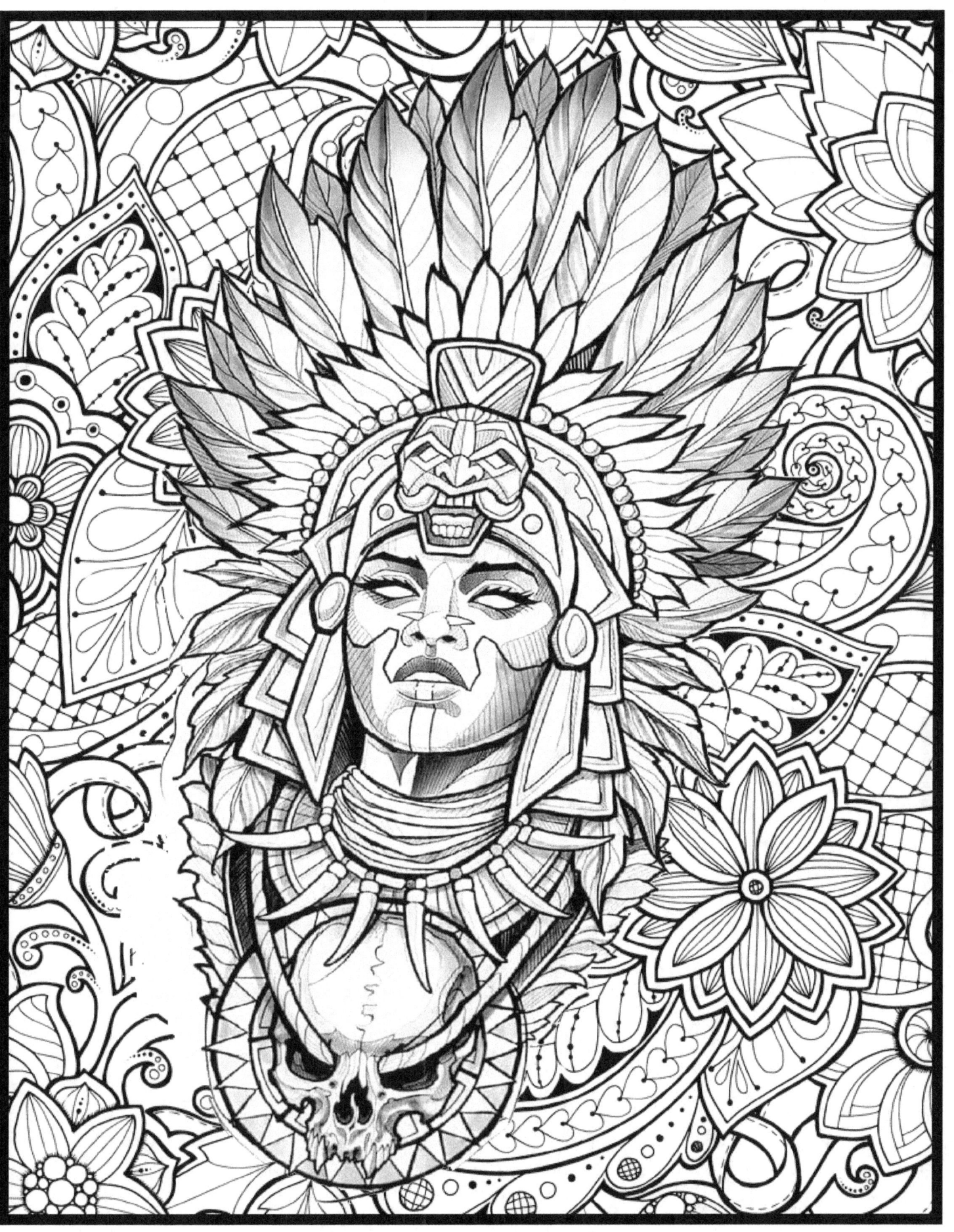

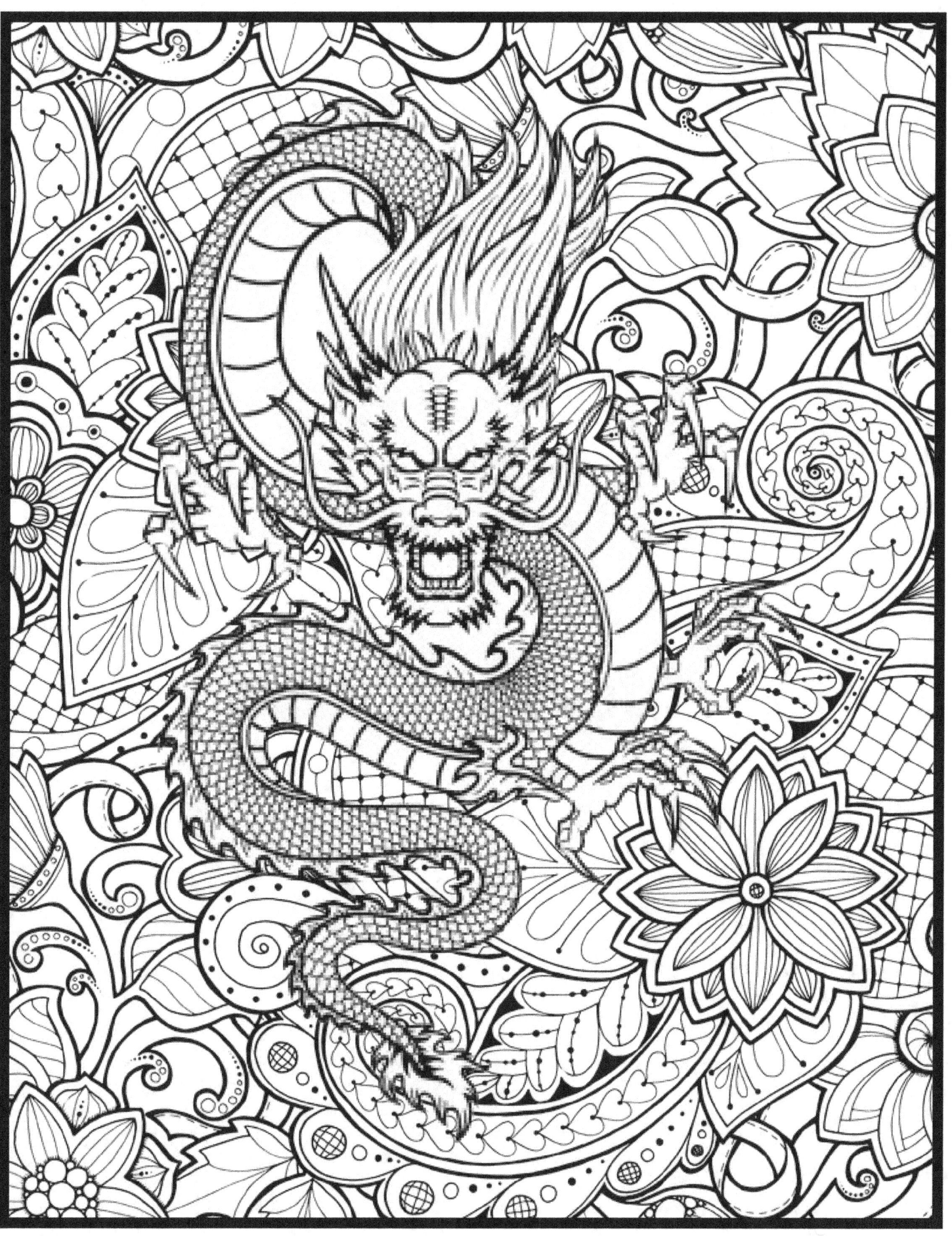

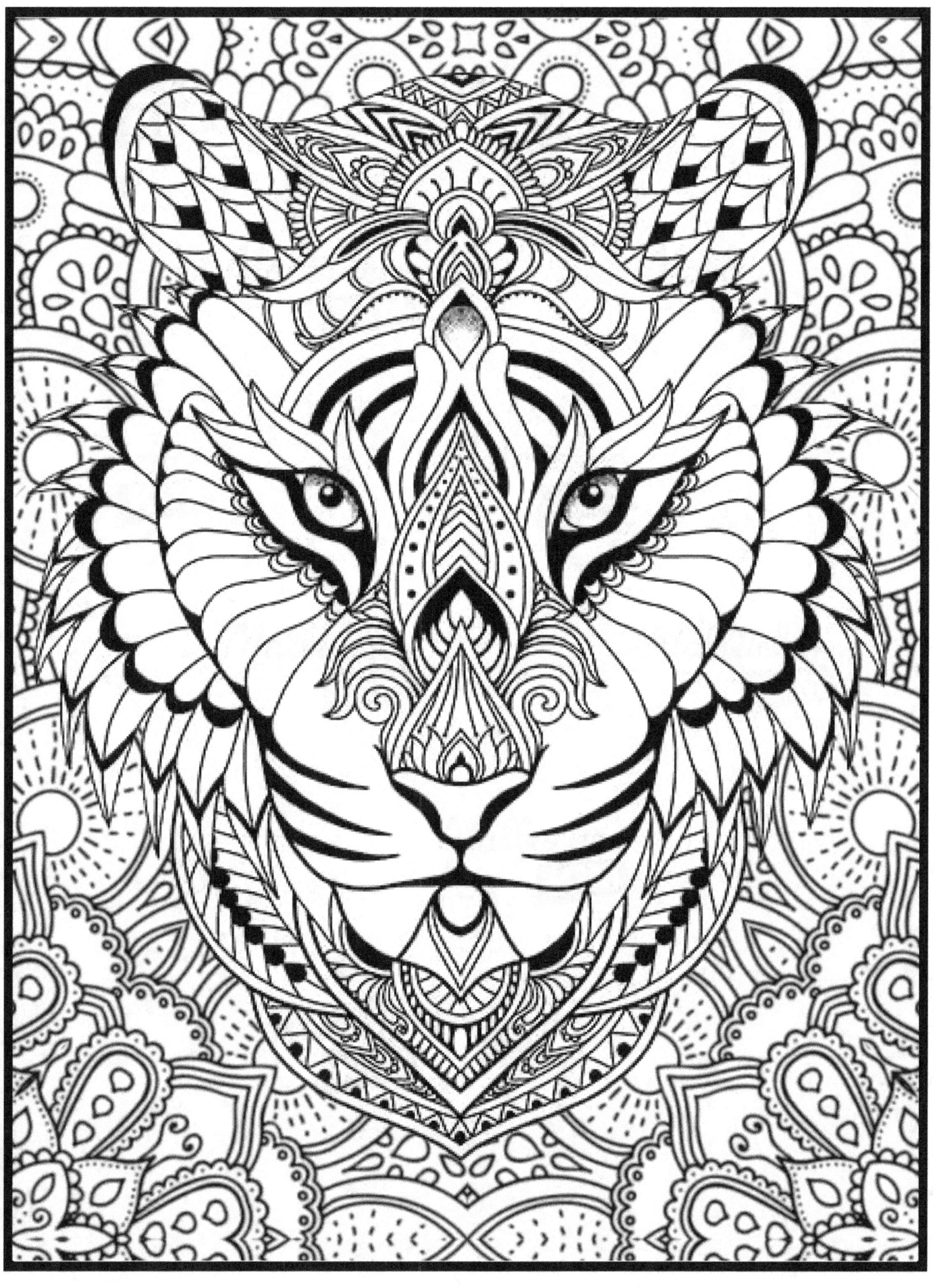

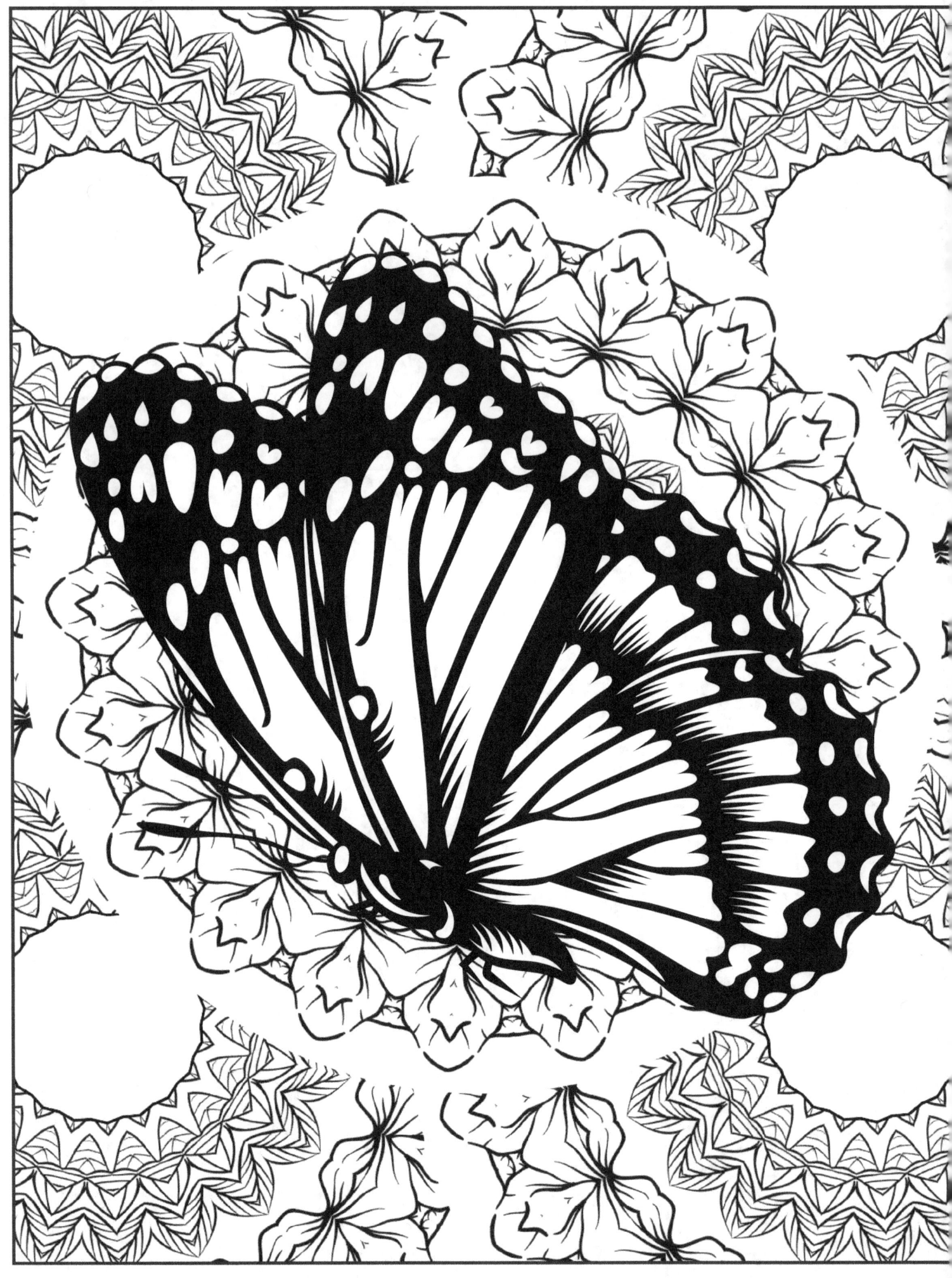

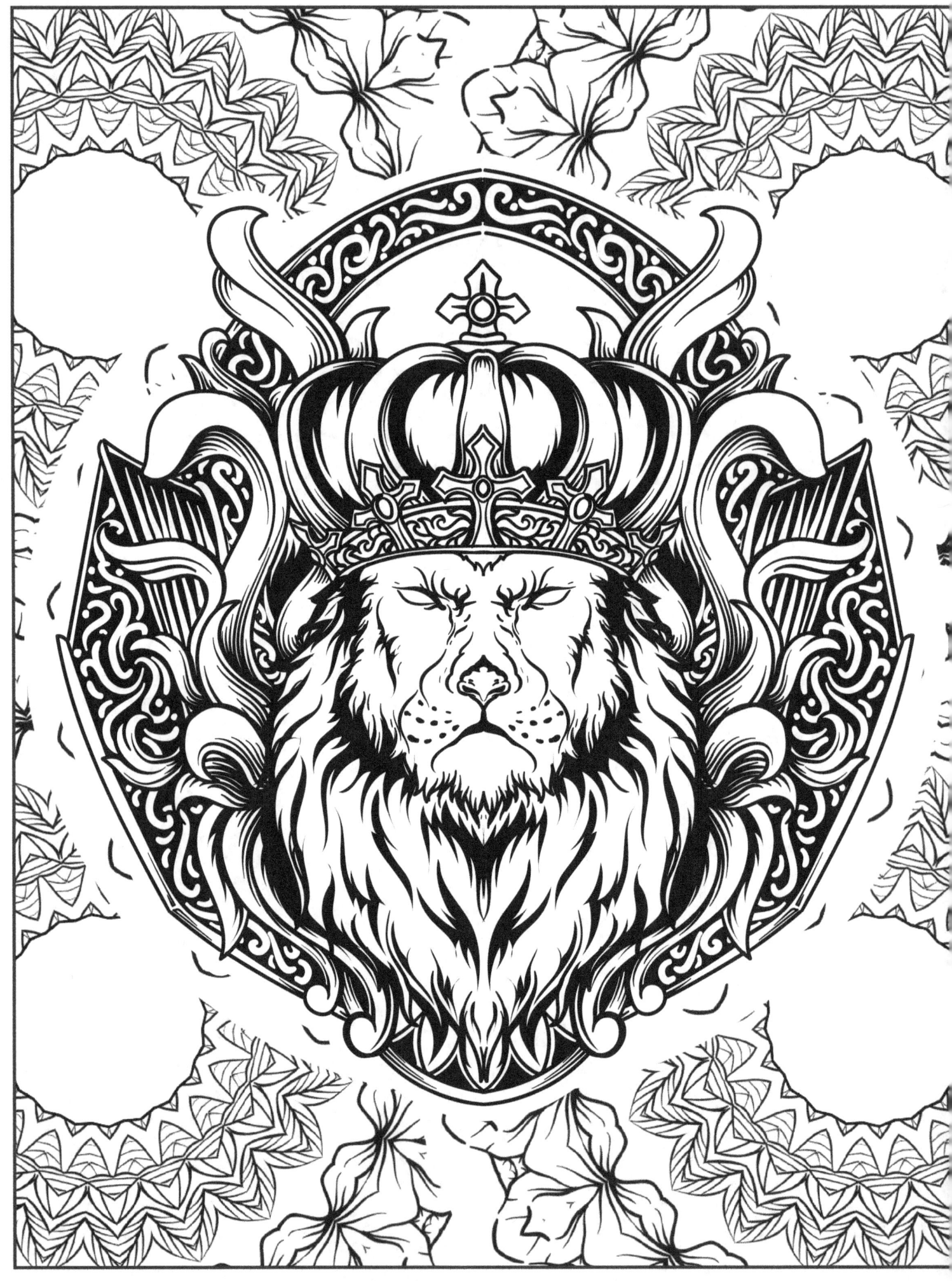

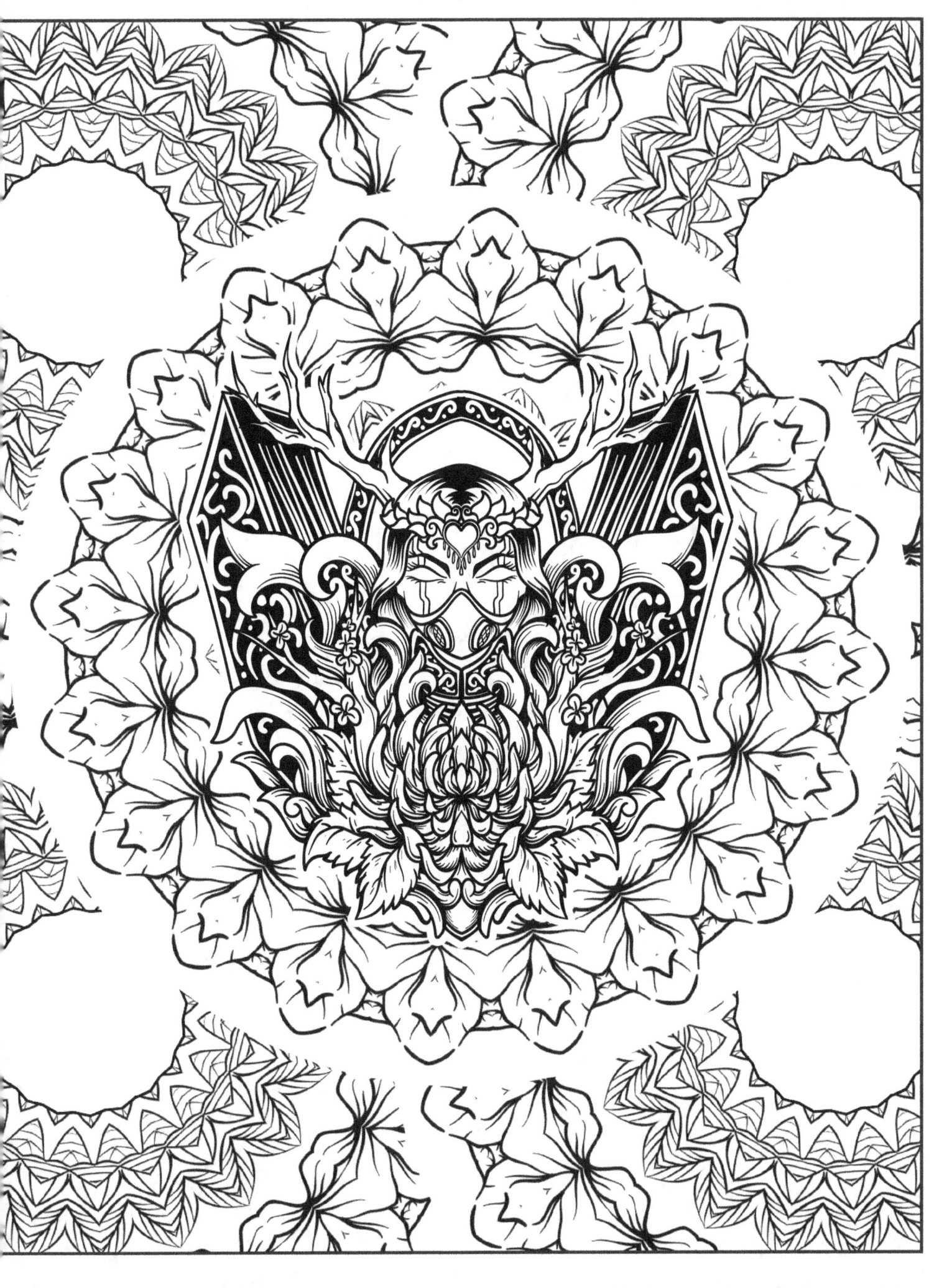

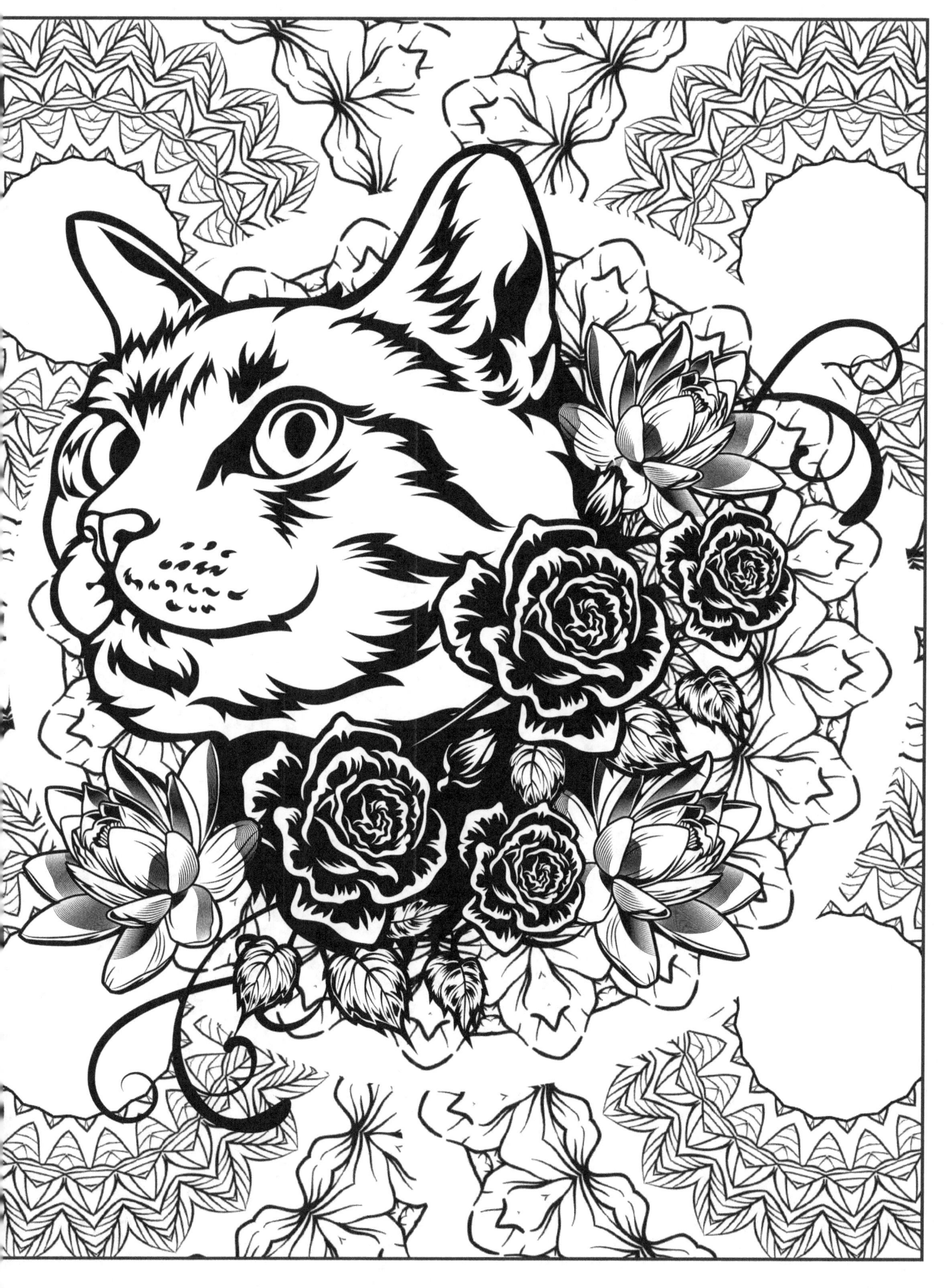

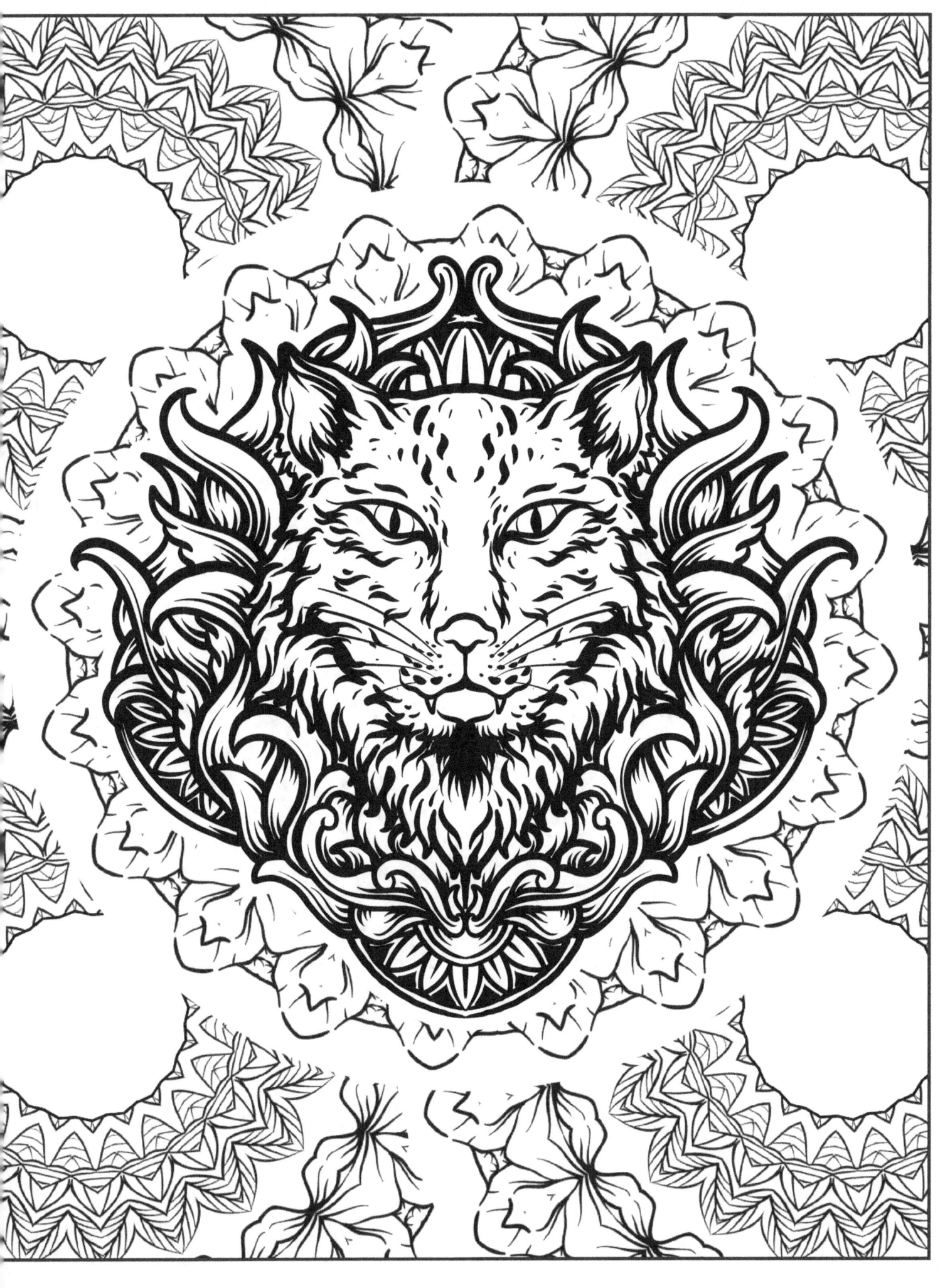

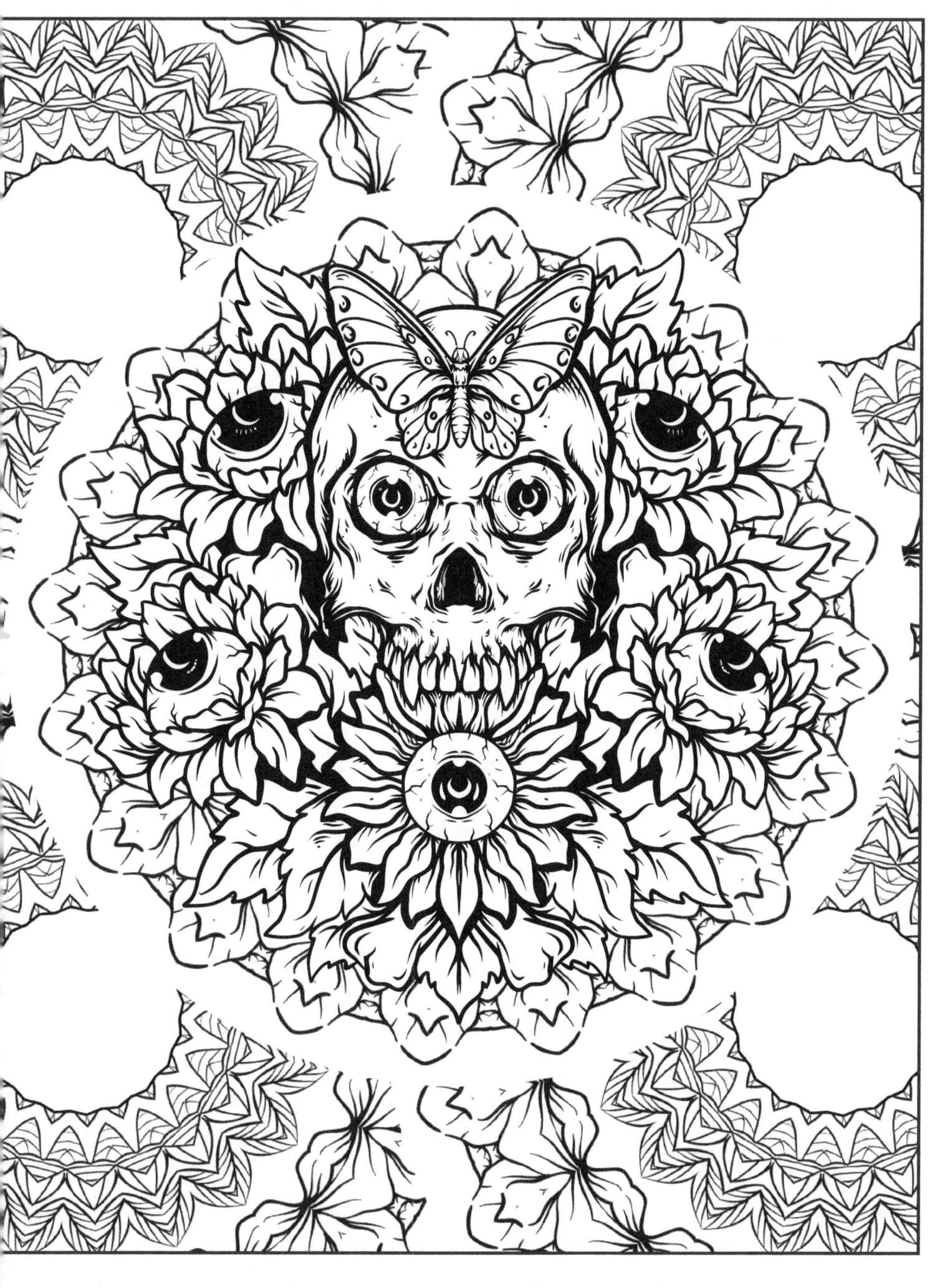

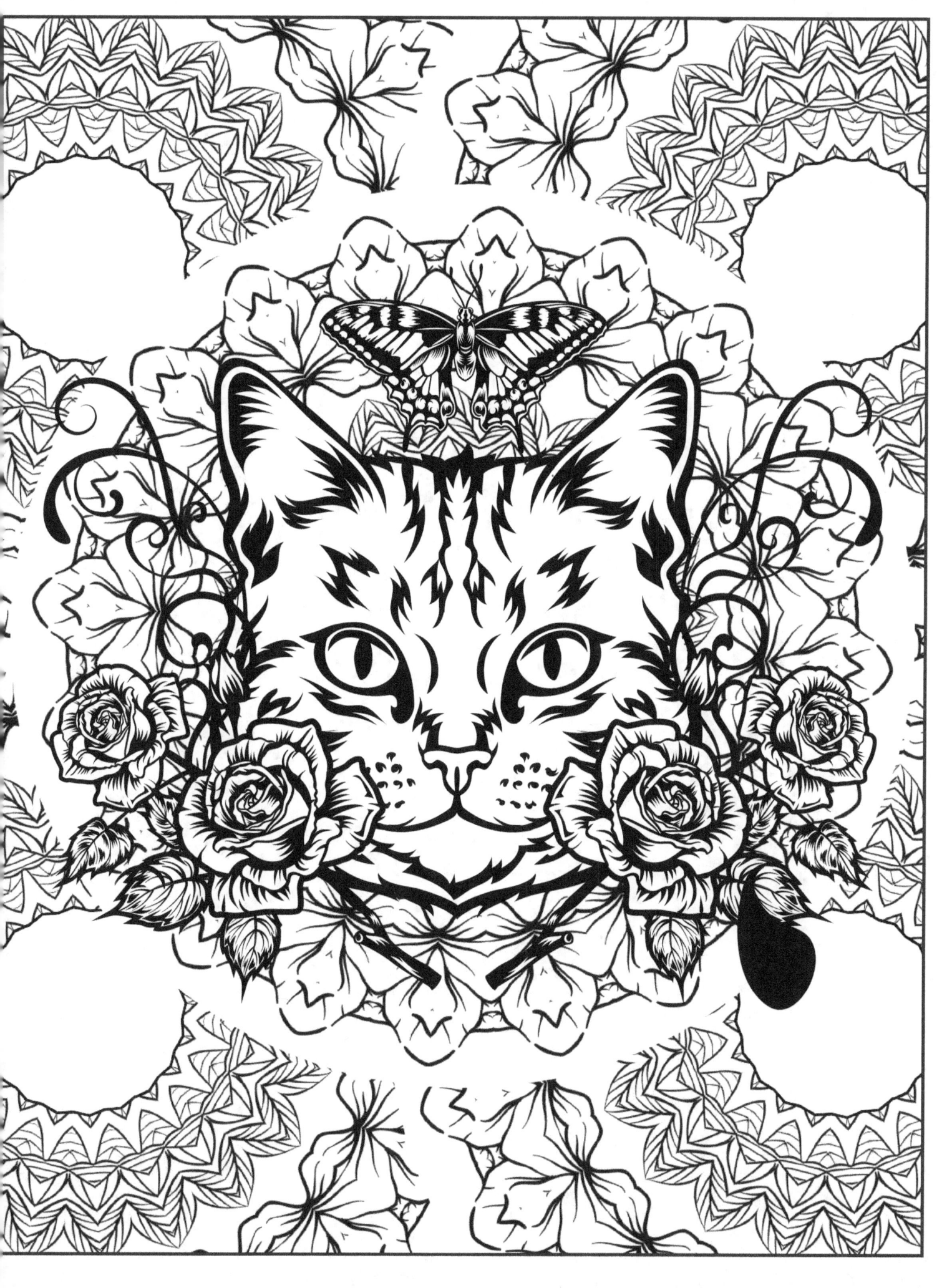

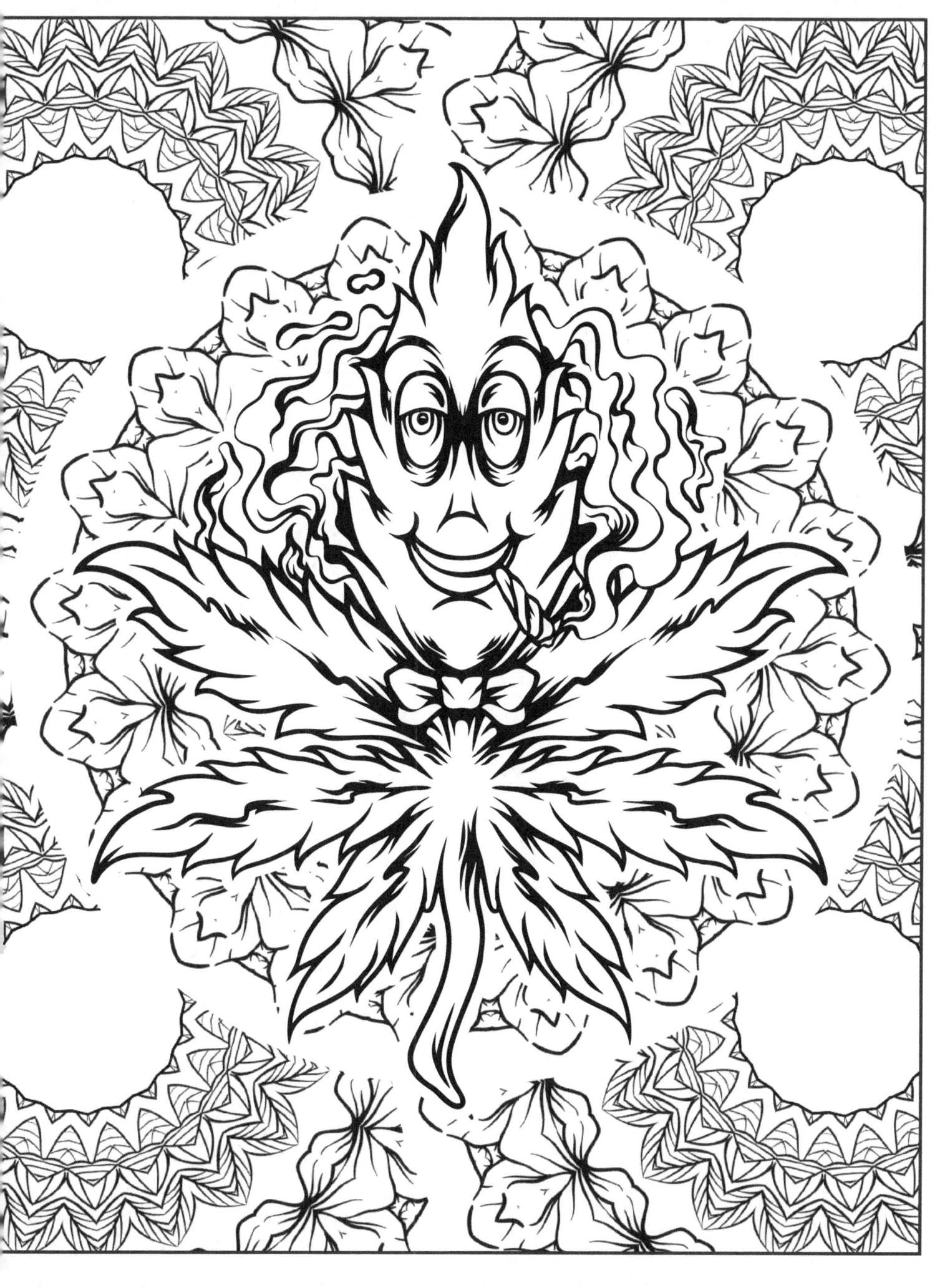

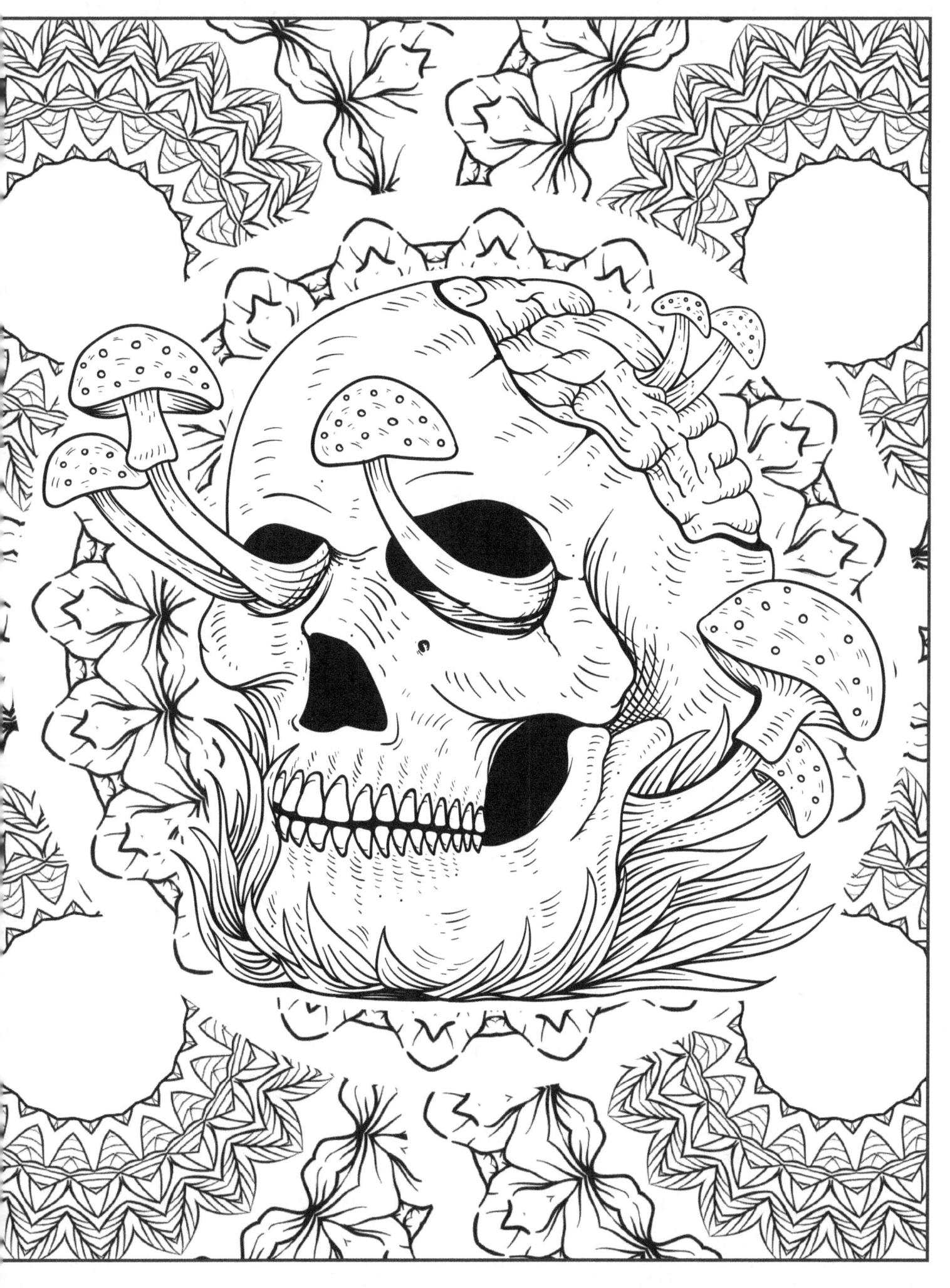

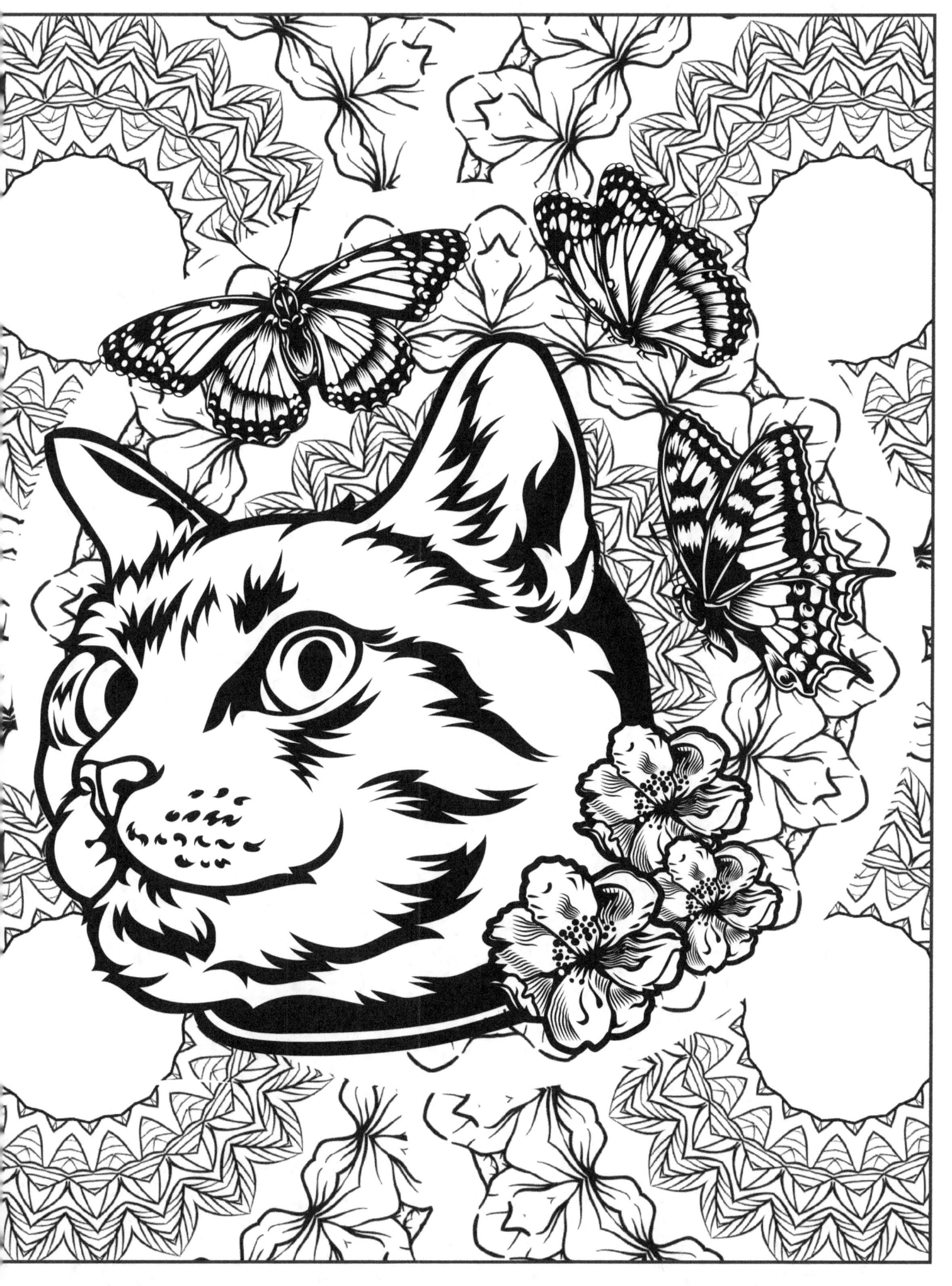

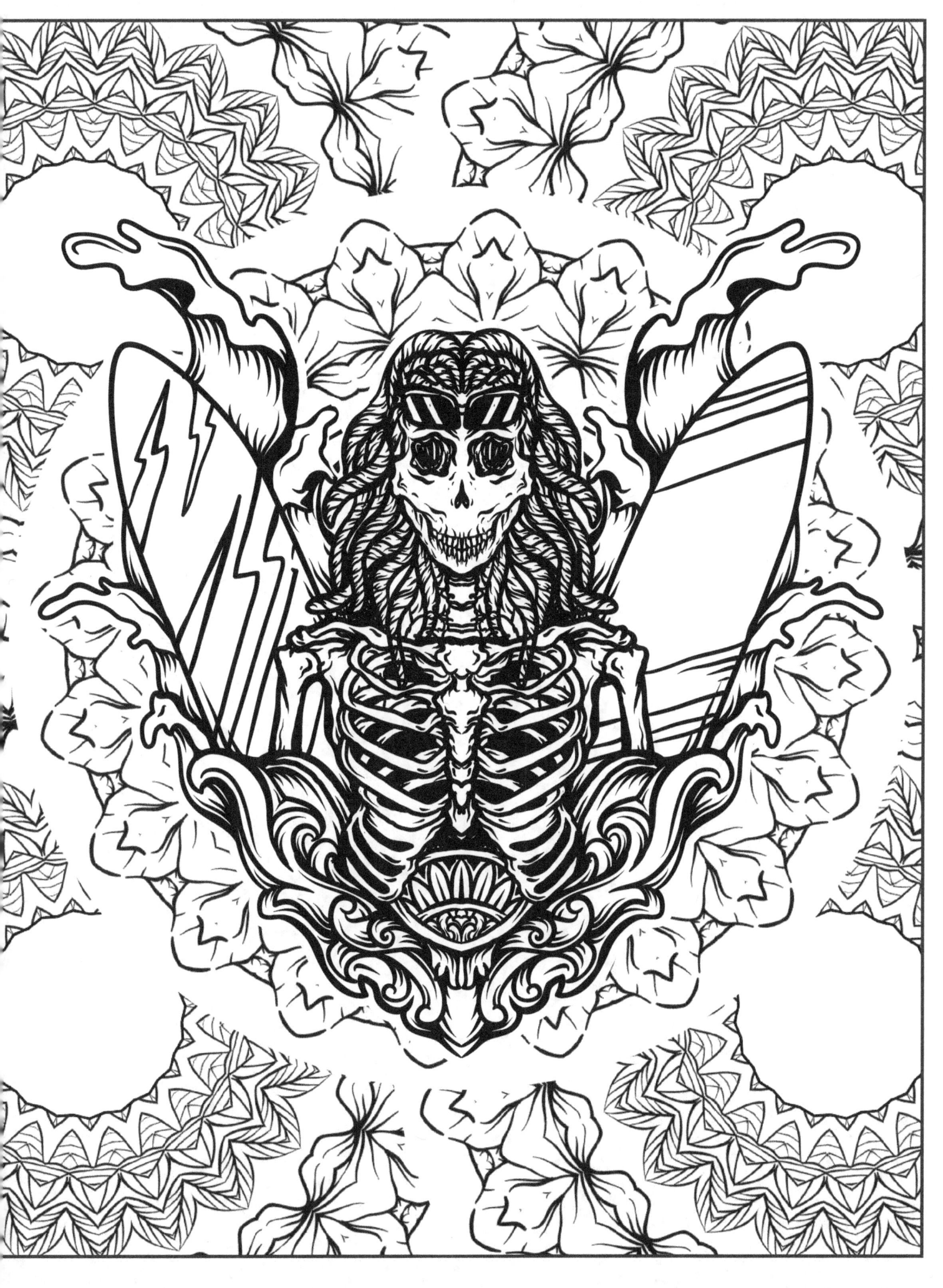

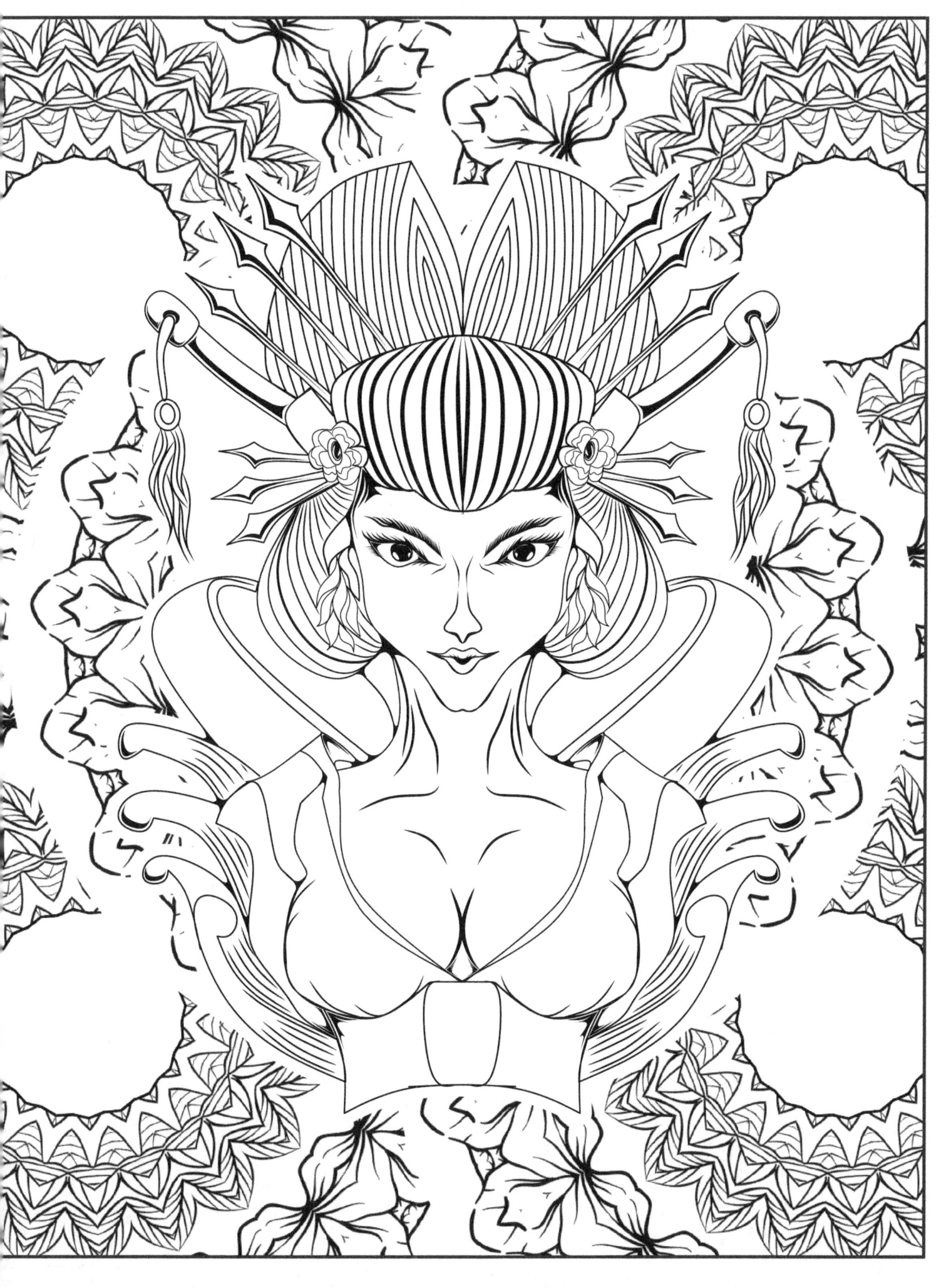

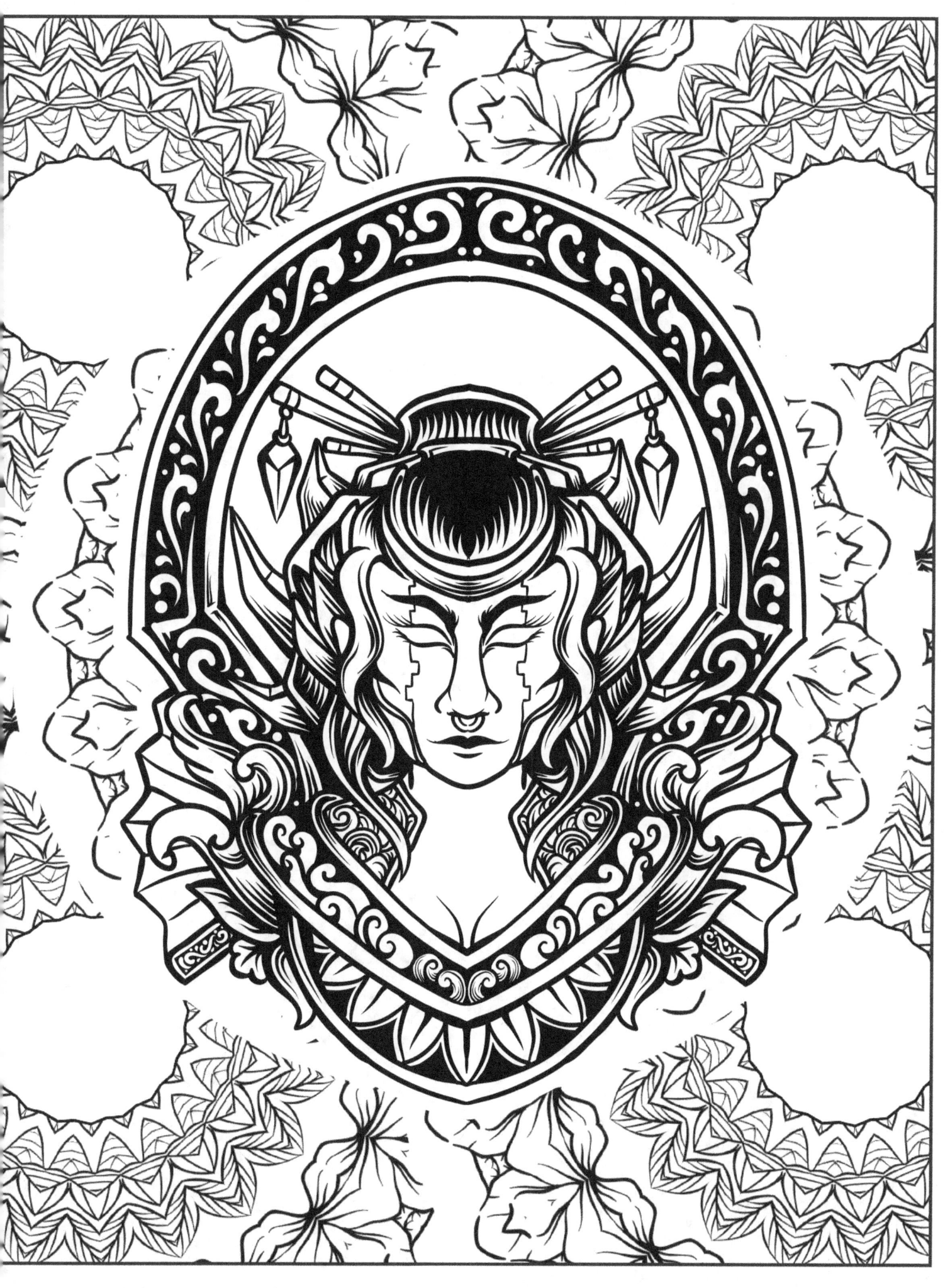

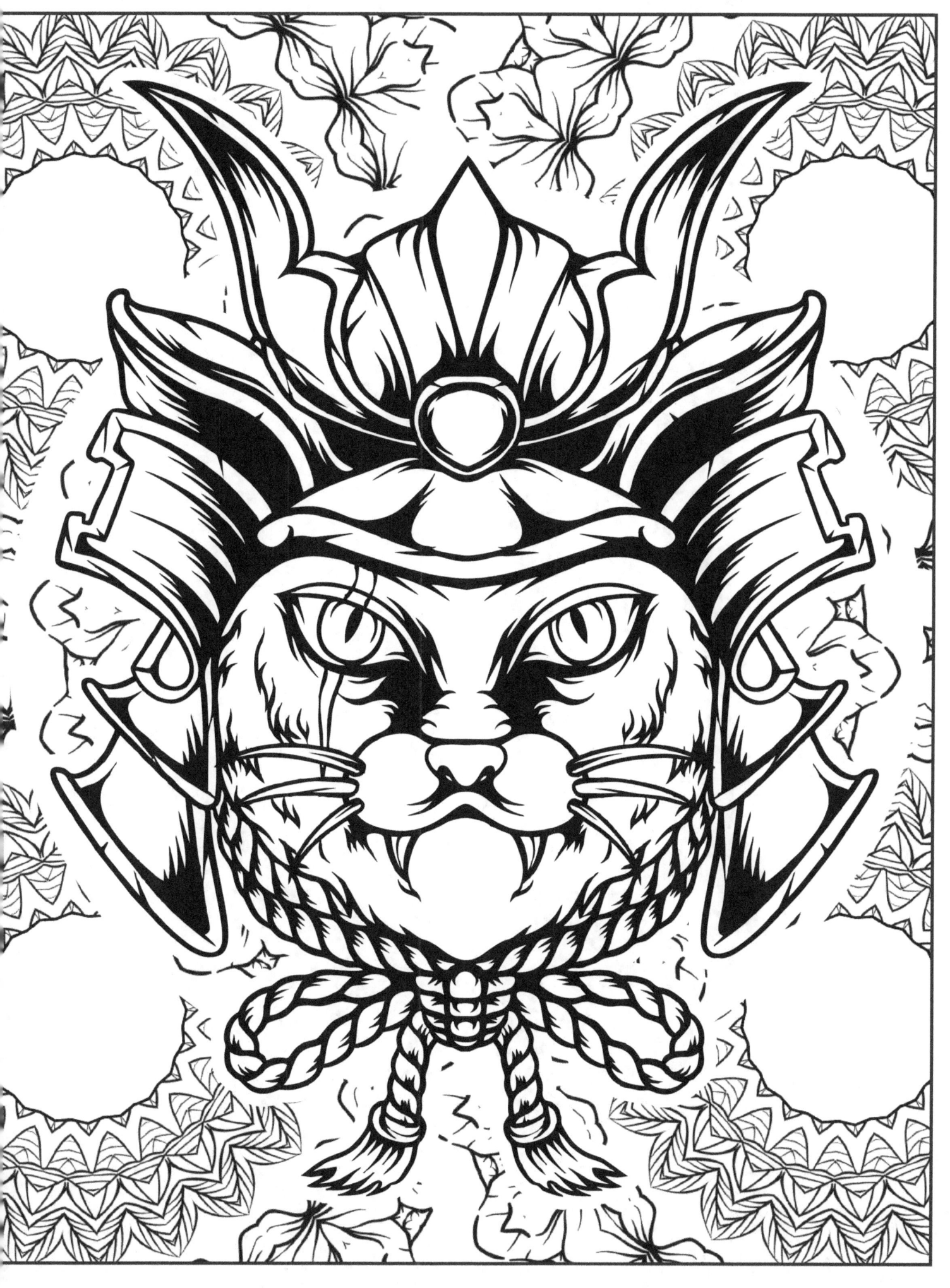

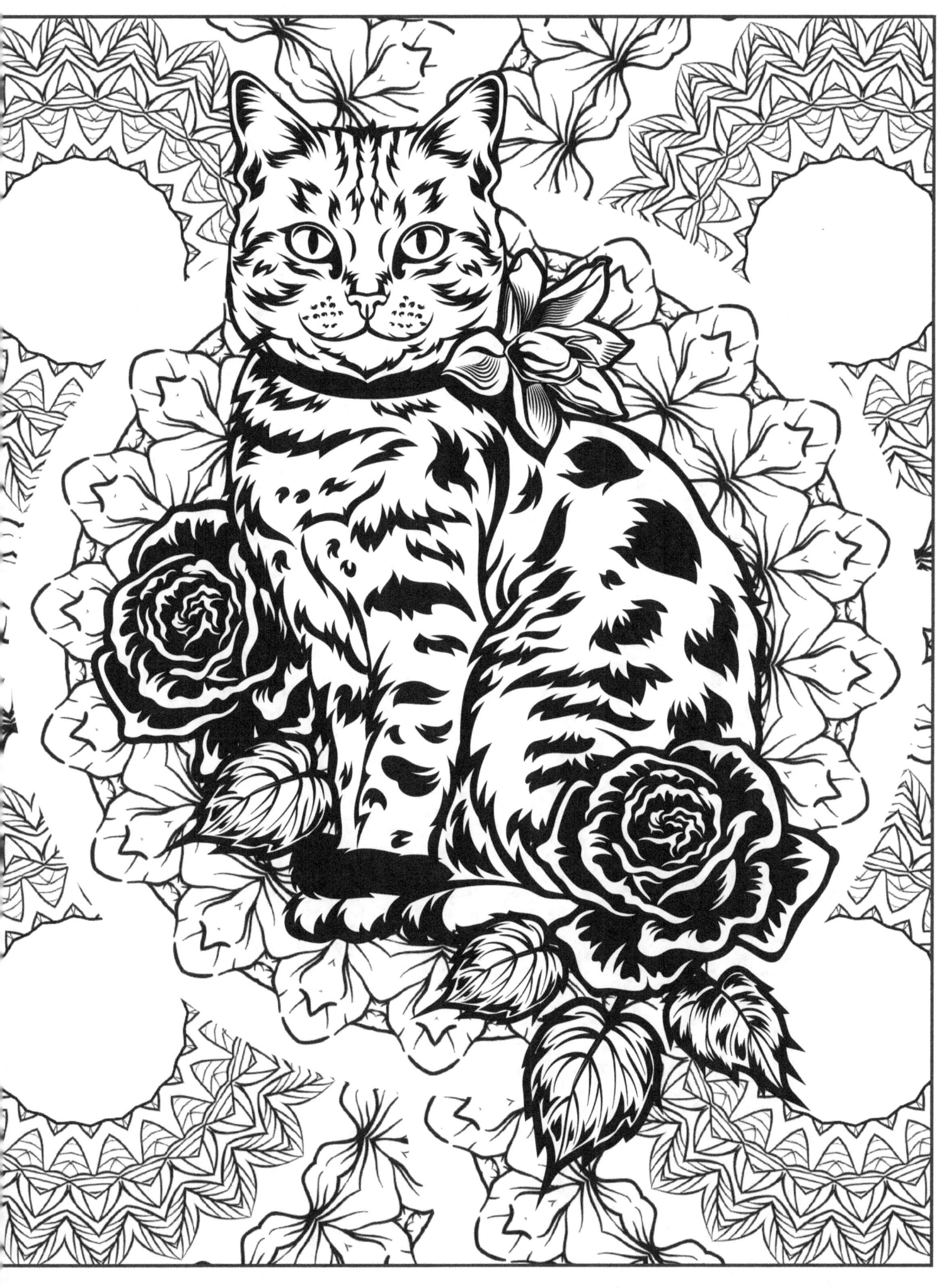

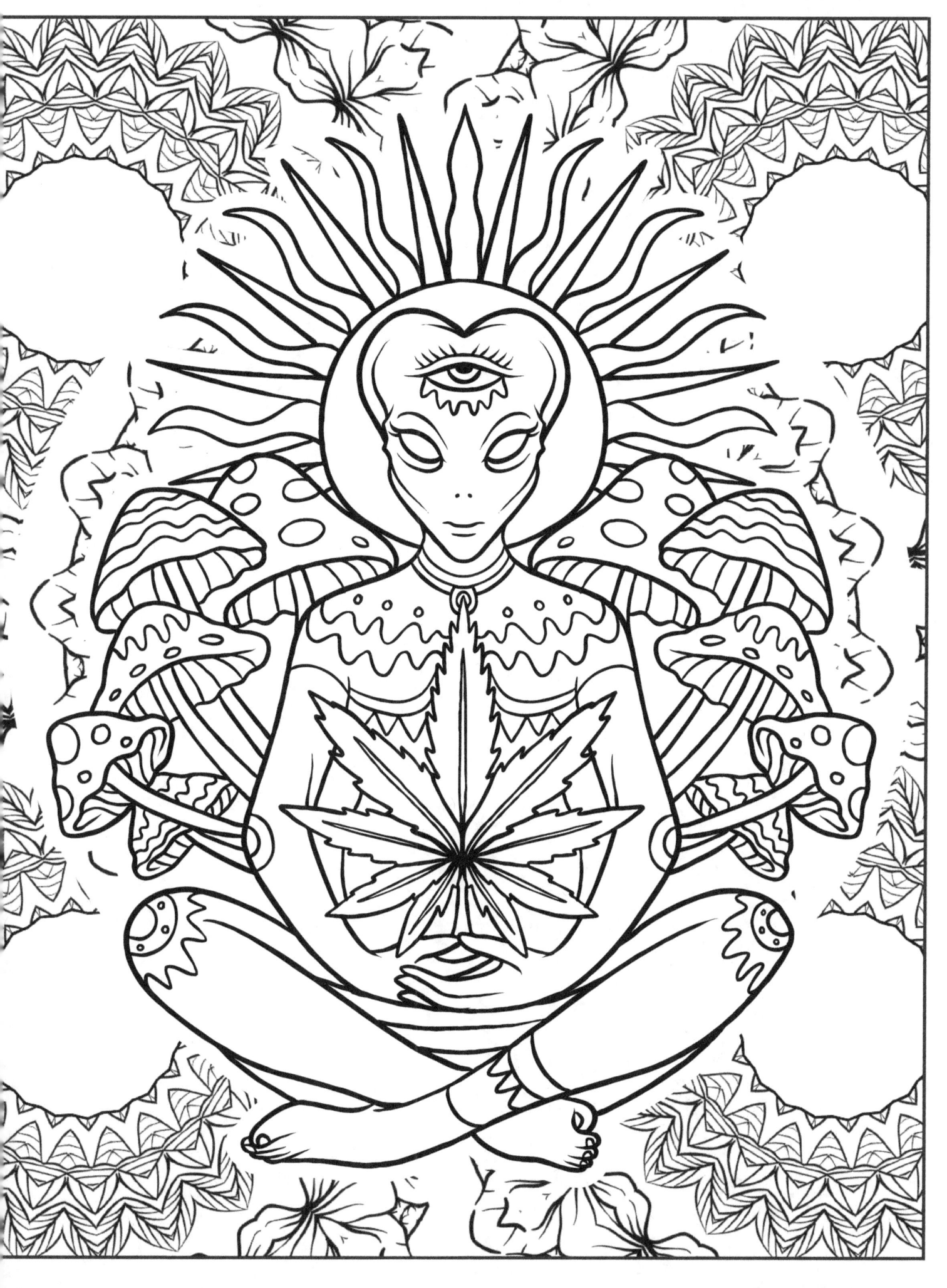

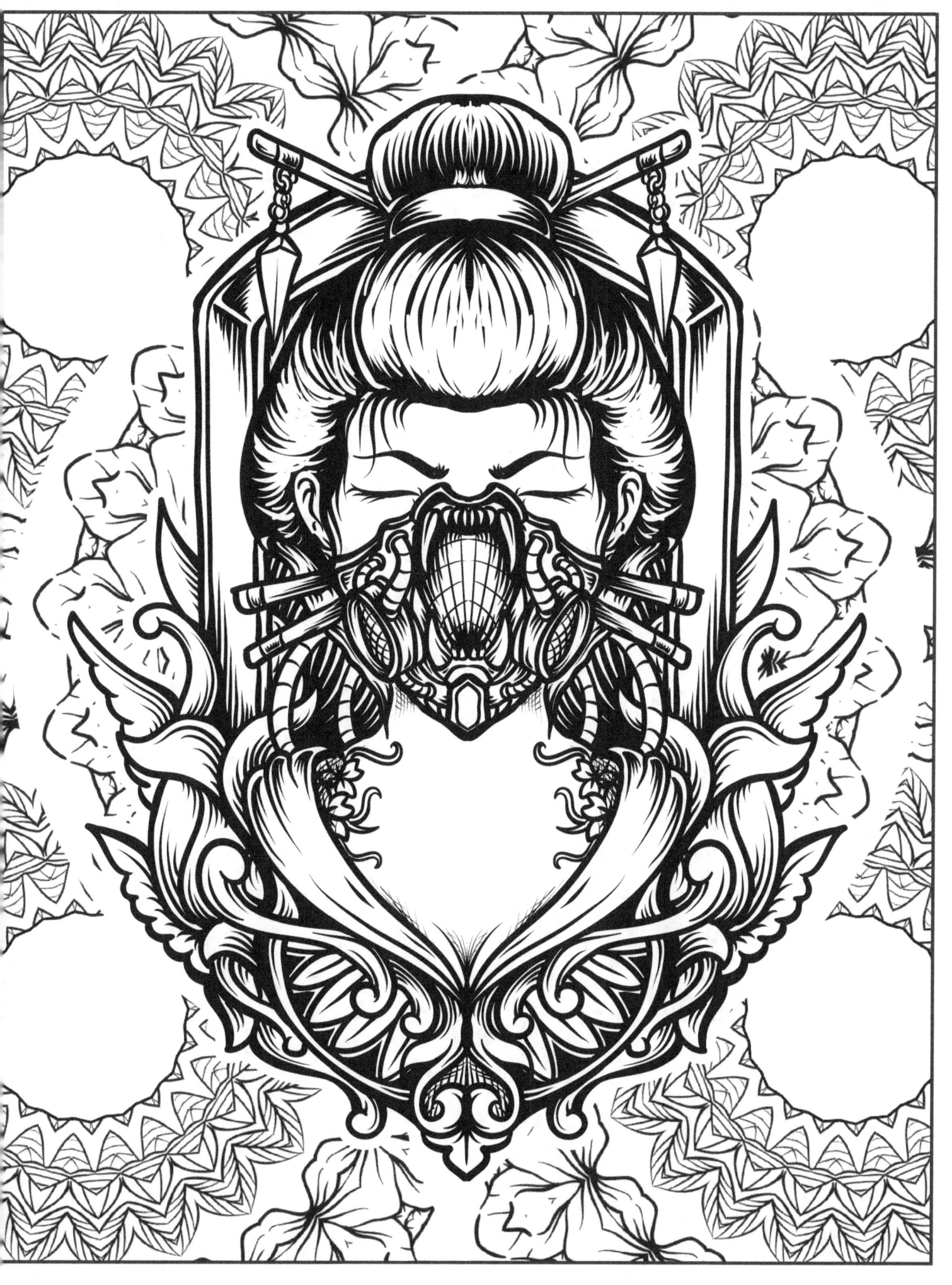

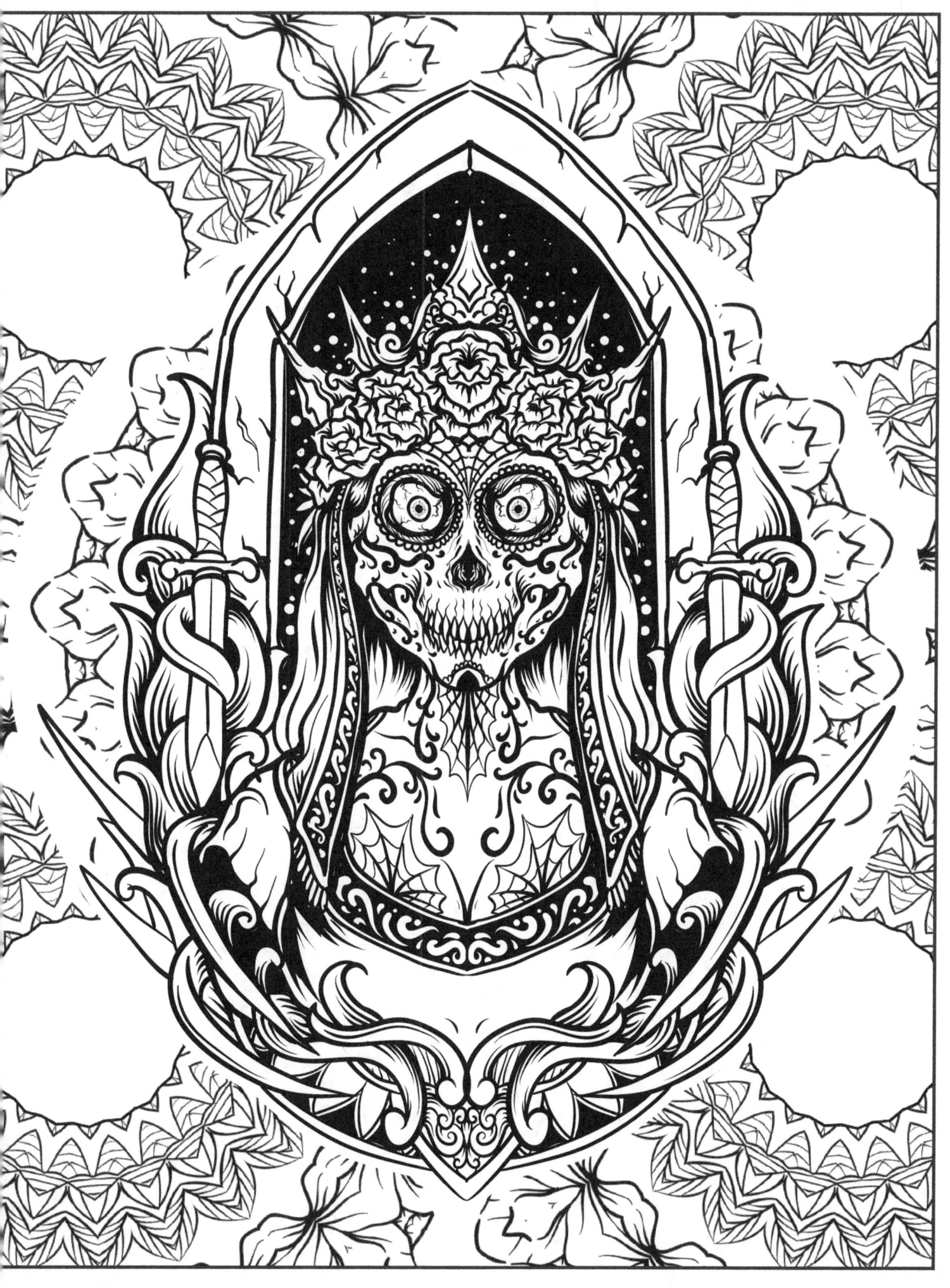

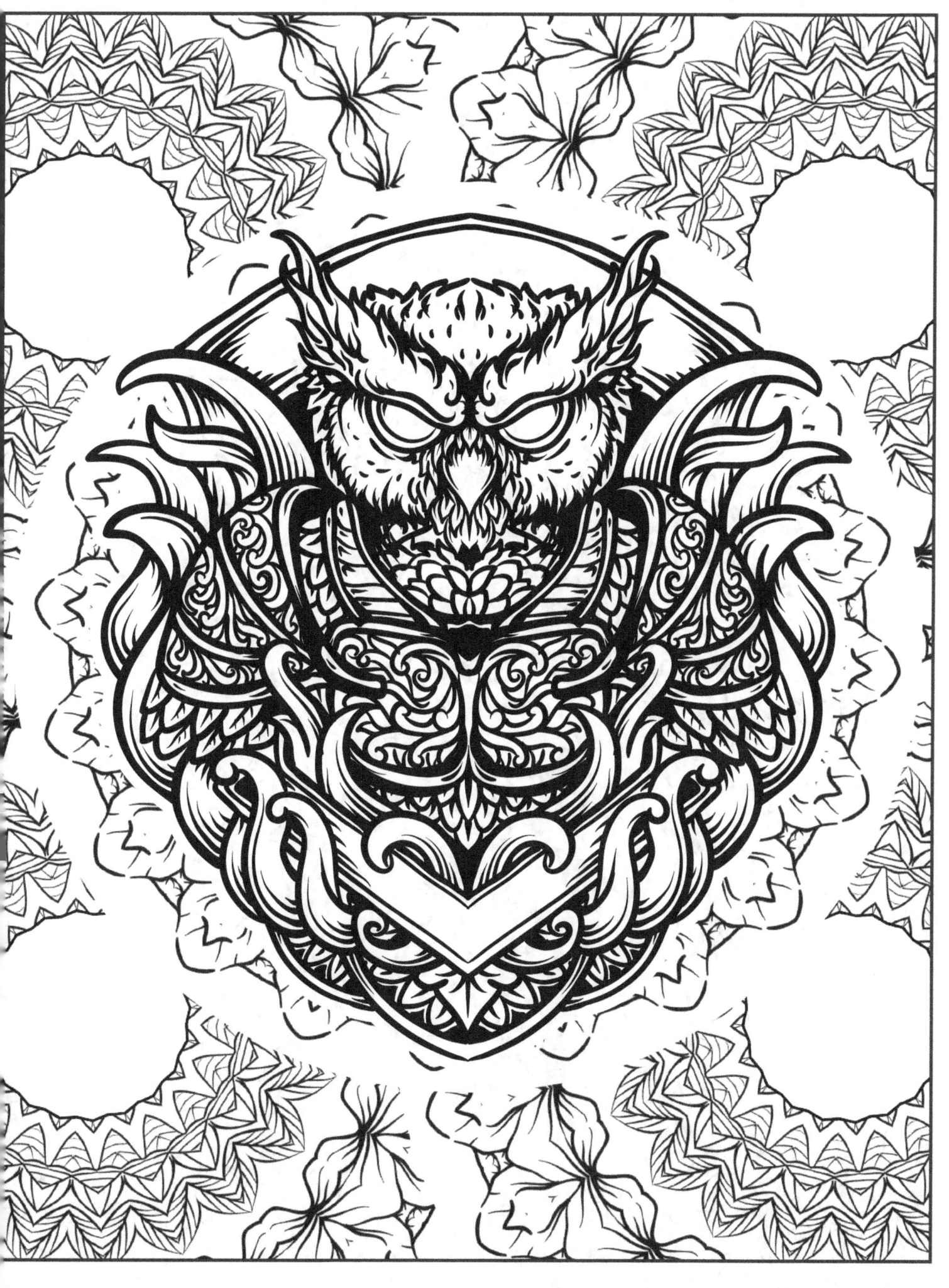

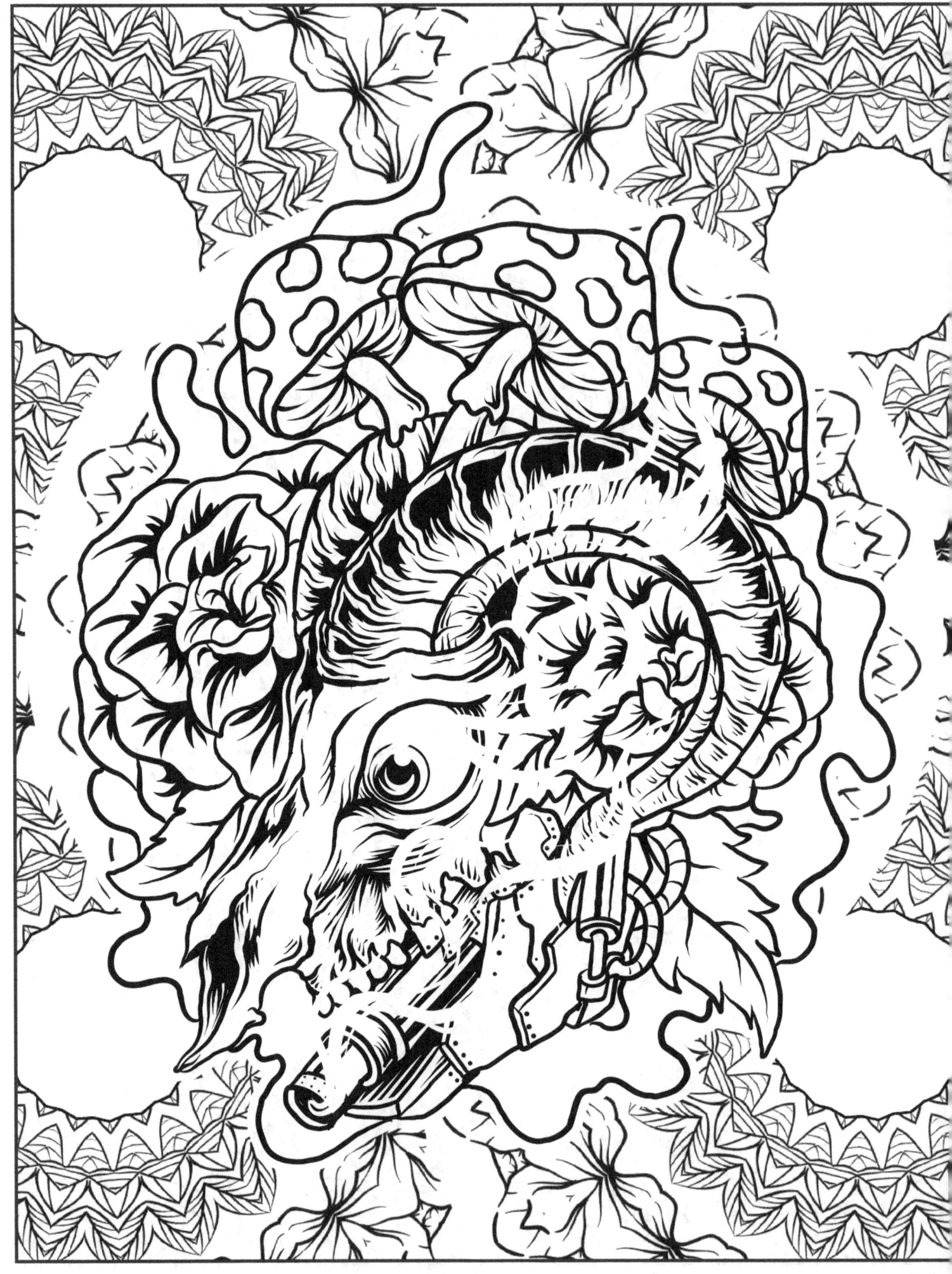

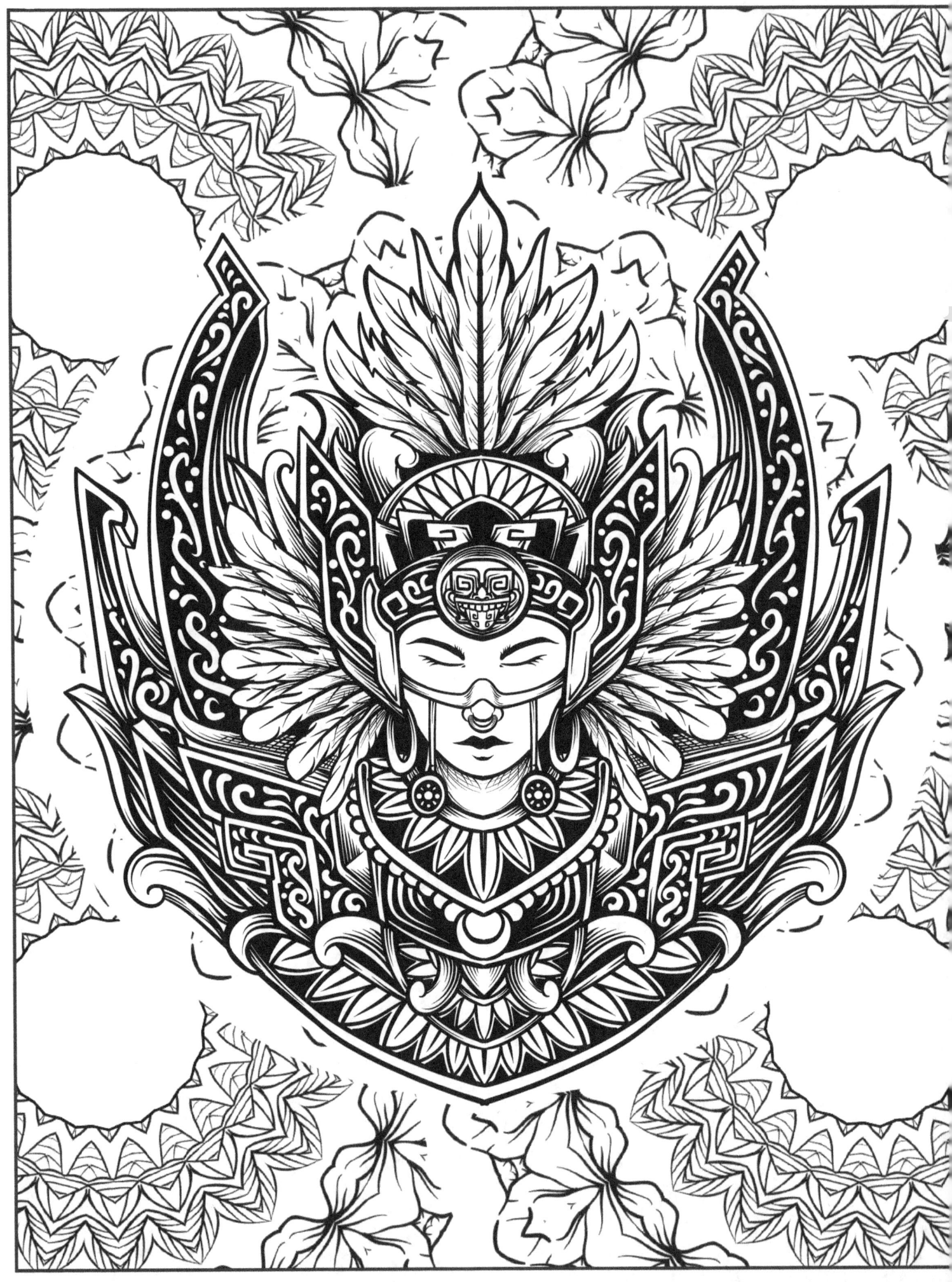

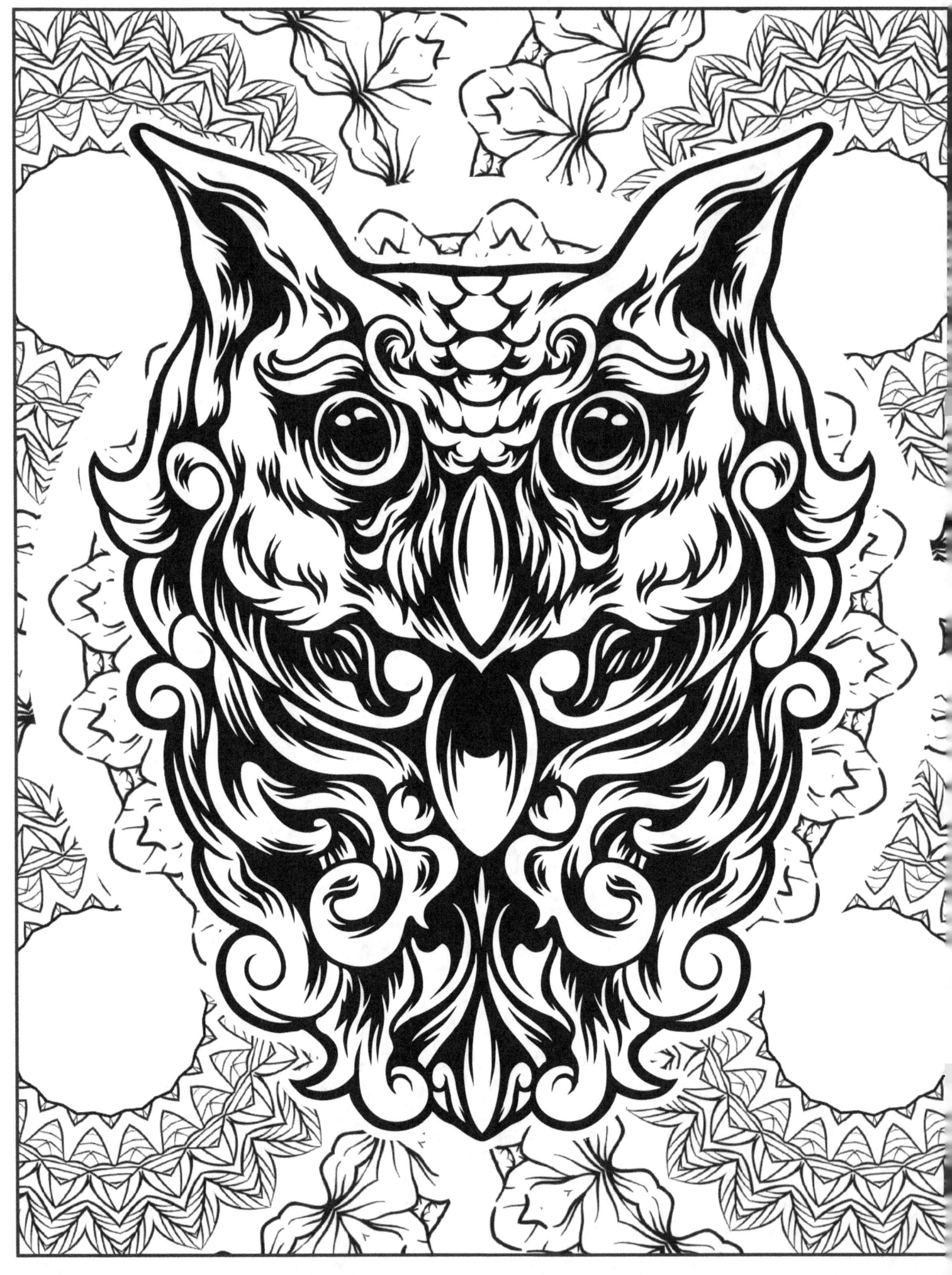

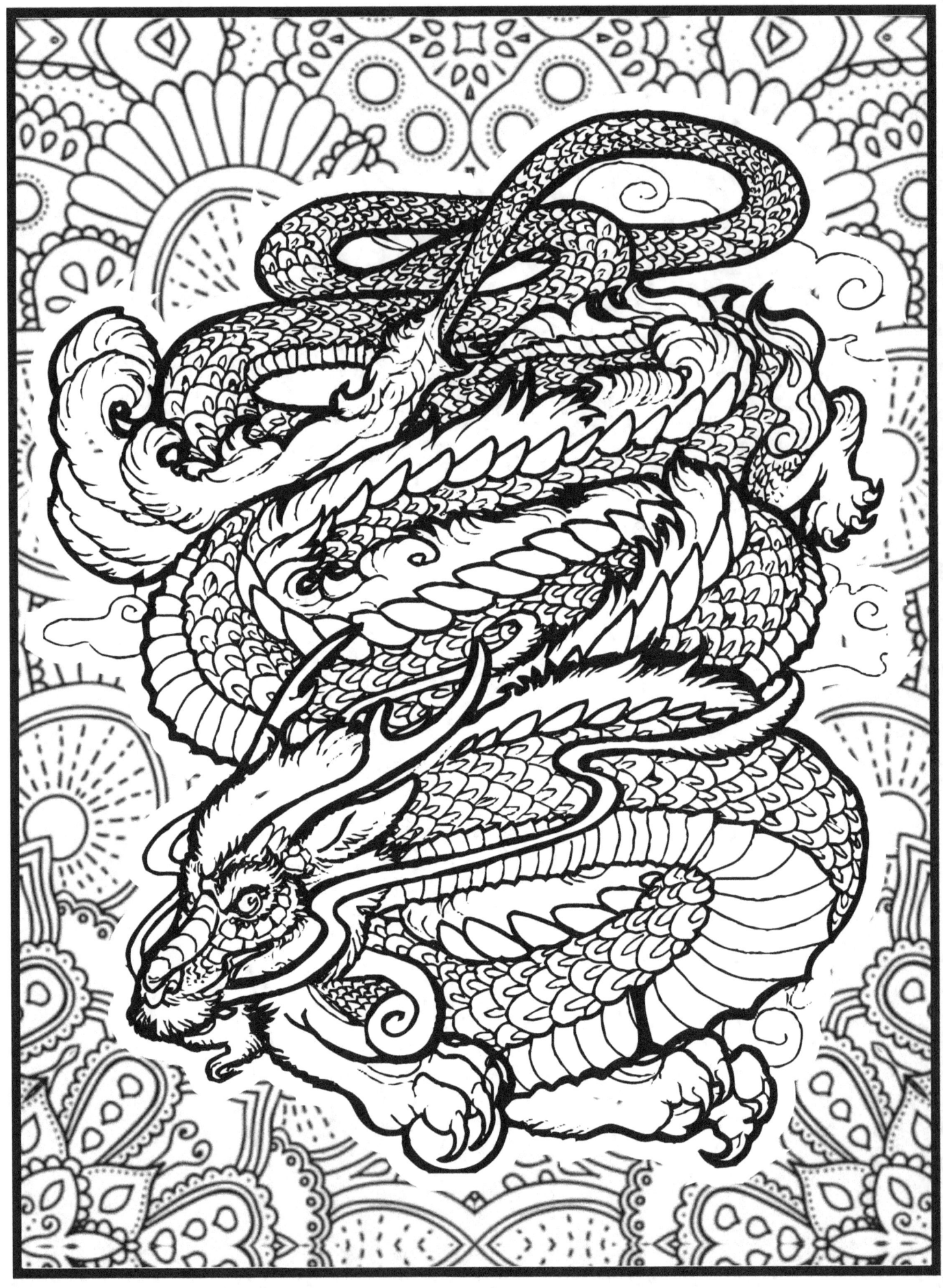